RESCUE SHOP

*Ten workshops to give Christians
the skills they need to
recover people for Jesus*

RESCUE SHOP

*Ten workshops to give Christians
the skills they need to
recover people for Jesus*

JOHN ALLAN

EXETER
THE PATERNOSTER PRESS

AUSTRALIA:
Bookhouse Australia Ltd.,
P.O. Box 115, Flemington Markets, NSW 2129

SOUTH AFRICA:
Oxford University Press,
P.O. Box 1141, Cape Town

British Library Cataloguing in Publication Data

Allan, John,
  Rescue shop.
  1. Christian church. Evangelism
  I. Title
  269'.2

  ISBN 0–85364–448–9

Typeset in Great Britain by
Photoprint, 9–11 Alexandra Lane, Torquay, Devon
and printed for The Paternoster Press,
Paternoster House, 3 Mount Radford Crescent, Exeter, Devon
by Cox & Wyman Ltd., Reading, Berks.

Contents

WORKSHOP 1

WORKSHOP 2

WORKSHOP 5

WORKSHOP 6

Introduction

Welcome to *Rescue Shop*. We've subtitled the book 'Ten workshops to give Christians the skills they need to recover people for Jesus'. Let me explain that description straight away.

Recover people? That's not how we usually describe evangelism. We have lots of other phrases which sound more familiar to Christian ears! But actually evangelism is all about 'recovery'. The non-Christian people whom we meet every day, with whom we share this planet, belong by rights to Jesus Christ. First of all, he made them, and they are accountable to him. Second, his death was on their behalf. As Paul put it, 'We are convinced that one died for all, and therefore all died.' Jesus Christ has rights over the life of every human being on this planet, and until those rights are recognised, life is not what it should be. Coming to Jesus Christ is like coming home. Evangelism is recovery.

It's important to see it this way, because so may ordinary Christians see 'personal witnessing' as something to be dreaded—as a religious exercise you occasionally perform upon your friends, which embarrasses both parties, but needs to be persisted with because it's in the Bible. Evangelism is not manipulation, or the application of an artificial technique. Evangelism isn't salesmanship. We aren't forcing upon our friends an ecclesiastical product they don't really want; we're simply inviting them to come home.

'*Skills*'? Now how does that fit with what I've just said? To talk about 'skills' suggests methods and gimmicks and doorstep selling ploys. But not really. In any form of human activity there are skills to be learnt—including the most personal areas, such as marriage and child-rearing. I'm still

1

learning marriage skills after twelve years at it, and I don't expect to graduate next week.

We have sometimes stressed the role of the Holy Spirit in evangelism to such an extent that Christians gain the impression that evangelism is some kind of remote-control magic. *If I just open my mouth, and say whatever pops into my head, the Holy Spirit will use it to bring my friends to the Lord.* And thus are produced half-baked testimonies, illogical arguments, emotional and unintelligible appeals. Unless we take the trouble to use the intelligence God has given us, and learn a few basic skills in relating to people and explaining ourselves naturally, why on earth should the Holy Spirit compensate for our laziness?

That leaves one word to explain. '*Workshops*'? Isn't that just a gimmicky name for another teaching session? Well, I hope not. The intention in producing this material has been that people should work on it *together*. The leader will teach the main points of each section, of course, but fairly briefly, and the real learning will come when people attempt the exercises planned into each workshop—exercises which involve them in using the ideas they have been taught, and absorbing them by putting them into action.

This means that the course doesn't require a tremendous amount of knowledge on the leader's part (and in case he wants to learn more, there are over fifty recommended books and back-up resources to supply him with extra reading for each workshop). All that it requires is a group of Christians who are concerned to make themselves as effective as they can be in the basic skills of recovering people for Jesus.

If that sounds like a fair description of your group—*Rescue Shop* is for you. I hope you'll enjoy it!

Guidelines for Leaders

Most of us learn how to share our faith in a pretty haphazard way. We pick up bits of good advice and helpful arguments from sermons and books we read. We learn by painful experience, in chatting to friends and neighbours, what to say and what not to say. We find our more from watching other people in action, and copying their good ideas. But there isn't much structure or system to it.

And then sometimes just before there is an evangelistic mission in our neighbourhood, the organizers make an appeal for counsellors, and we find ourselves press-ganged into a lightning course in How to Share Your Faith and How to Lead A Person to Christ. We earnestly memorize all the little verses we're given and march around in a state of militant preparedness for a few days. Then the mission goes by—and we start forgetting all we ever knew.

The danger of haphazard learning is that we may never totally understand what we're trying to do. We never take the job apart, component by component, and examine it systematically. And the danger of lightning courses is that we can end up with a few gimmicks and a supposedly sure-fire technique—which will work in some situations and not in others. We end up presenting people with what Jim Petersen has called 'the Gospel of the Christian contract':

> Possibly the most common weakness in our contemporary approach to evangelism is our tendency to focus our message on the Christian contract—how to transact a relationship with God—rather than on the person of Jesus Christ. We become so intent on helping someone understand how to put his faith in Christ that we overlook the very real probability that he is almost devoid in his knowledge of Jesus Christ . . .

> We tend to become more interested in responses than in
> *understanding*. We strive to elicit agreement, and once it is
> achieved we seek to extract a positive response. We call this
> 'making a decision'. This is the forced contract. (Jim Petersen,
> *Evangelism for Our Generation*. Navpress.)

It's been good that over the last few years there has been a
new world-wide emphasis on what has come to be called
'lifestyle evangelism'—the skill of being able to share our
faith in Jesus Christ quite naturally, *as an ongoing activity*, not
just at special times of mission or outreach. I'm convinced
that this is vital for at least two reasons. First, by far the
majority of new Christians find faith through personal conversation with one other person—it's outstandingly the most
effective form of witness. Second, the best opportunities to
share your faith meaningfully will happen to you unexpec-
tedly, in the ordinary circumstances of daily life; and *not*
usually in the artificial, hectic atmosphere of a special
mission.

Not that I'm knocking missions. I've spent over a decade
organizing and leading them! But everything I've ever done
has convinced me that it's on the personal, one-to-one level
that most good will be achieved. And hence this course. I
hope it will help Christians to look seriously at *everything*
that's involved in true, responsible witness, and sharpen the
skills necessary for them to be most effective in ordinary
living for Jesus Christ.

HOW IT WORKS

This course will help you organize training workshops for a
small group of people—such as a Christian Union group, a
home Bible study, a church cell group or youth group or
men's group—who want to learn to evangelize more effectively (or indeed, learn to do it for the very first time). You
may feel quite unconfident about your ability to lead such
sessions—after all, you're hardly Billy Graham yourself—but
don't worry. The original material was written for the young
people of a group of churches in Poland, where principles of
evangelism have often to be taught to remote groups many

miles distant from the nearest Bible teacher! So it's presented in what (I hope) will be a fairly 'idiot-proof' style, and all the necessary resources, answers, hints and advice are supplied for you.

You can of course chop and change the course to suit yourself. There is a great deal of flexibility built in, and for example you will have to choose just some of the ninety or so group exercises which are supplied. You may want to cut down the number of sessions (but think hard before you do— each one is very important) or take things at a slower pace, spending more than one meeting on each. A typical session should fit quite comfortably into an hour, but you may find you can shorten or lengthen it. The course has sometimes been taught intensively over a weekend or a couple of weekends, and although this is not ideal it is possible for people to benefit from it in such a way. A college CU group, for instance, might find that it could form the basis for a very effective pre-mission weekend together.

If you don't want to undertake the full course, but simply run one or two workshops on areas which are of especial strategic interest to your group, that's possible too. Each workshop will stand on its own (except that it's not a good idea to tackle 4 without 5, or vice versa).

For new Christians, the course provides a simple introduction to things they need to know. For those more experienced, the course puts in order principles and facts which they may have known for some time, and breaks them down in an understandable way to make them easy to remember. Generally speaking, groups with less knowledge and experience may find some of the more demanding workshops (3, 4, 5 and 9) need more than one group meeting to cover the material. Groups with a lot of background understanding may not need to spend so long on workshops 1, 7 and 8.

MAKE IT INTERESTING

You will find that people can have a lot of fun in these workshops. Not that you're doing it for that reason, of course; but you will find that humour keeps on intruding quite naturally. That's because evangelism is potentially quite an embarrassing thing; it puts us in situations sometimes where all our social skills are taxed; and one obvious escape route from embarrassment is to laugh at it. Now that can be useful to you. I've found that when people laugh, they tend to learn. Make it enjoyable for them.

Do not treat the material as a sermon to be preached by the leader. Break up the workshops with exercises and group discussions (you'll find plenty of suggestions in the directions for each session, but don't feel restricted to just those). If the group is small, encourage participation and the asking of questions. Move at the pace the group can manage— don't be in a hurry to reach the end. Between workshops, set homework assignments (again, we suggest ideas), so that people can try out what they have learned in theory. At the beginning of each workshop, ask people to report back on their homework. (This of course doesn't apply if you're telescoping the material into one weekend . . . which is a drawback you must think about carefully.)

WHAT MEMBERS WILL NEED

People remember things more easily if they are presented in a variety of ways which reinforce one another. And so the teaching of the workshop is designed to come to them in three ways simultaneously:

(a) what you tell them, and they discuss together;
(b) visual aids which make your main points clear;
(c) the course notebook, which contains outline notes for the material that will be covered in the workshops.

This means, of course, that everyone needs a copy of the course notebook. If you turn to the back of this book, you will find some important pages (2–25), which you have our permission to photocopy, as much as you need to. This is the course notebook. You can decide for yourself whether you want to give the group a copy of the whole thing at the start of the course (snag: no element of surprise about what's coming next) or dole it out in individual sheets each time you meet (snag: at least one third of them can be relied on to lose vital bits of it before the course is over).

The notebook gives them no more than main headings and a few diagrams. This is so that they will add their *own* notes to those in the book, rather than having it all done for them. And so they should bring a pen each time, plus probably some extra paper. Each person will also need a Bible for some—if not all—of the workshops. Explain that everybody must attend *all* workshops; each part counts.

YOUR PREPARATION

Take time before each workshop to pray carefully. READ through the teaching material, and all Scripture references given, until you are sure you understand it and are familiar with it. Make notes of the main points as you go along. PREPARE any extra materials, visual aids, and the like, well in advance. PLAN exactly how long you will spend on each part of the session (you may well have to change your plans if the meeting doesn't go as you envisage, but never mind— make a plan anyway!) THINK of any illustrations you wish to include from your own personal experience, or from books you have read. And PRAY for each member of your group, by name, asking God to make the next workshop an important time of learning for that person.

VISUAL AIDS

The kind of visual aids you use will depend on the equipment available to you, and the size of the group. For large groups, overhead projector transparencies are ideal; or you could draw diagrams on a blackboard as you go along (except for a few complex ones which would have to be prepared in advance). For small groups, a large block of drawing paper with the diagrams drawn on successive pages could be used as a flip-chart. If you want to use something really permanent and impressive, buy a Nyrex folder with transparent windows, such as reps use to demonstrate their wares. Choose whichever method suits you, but do make it visual; people remember much more of what they *see* than of what they only *hear*.

EXERCISES

Choose the group exercises and activities with care, to suit the people you are teaching. Those with special abilities (e.g. an aptitude for drama, or the gift of getting others involved in games) may be useful to you in helping to motivate the others. Remember that older people will be less willing to join in unfamiliar activities; they don't have the flexibility of youth. On the other hand, younger teenagers, who are easily embarrassed, could become very shy and uncooperative if you asked them to do something too unusual early in the course, before they had gained confidence. The emphasis at the start should be on getting people to open themselves up to the others in the group, to establish the kind of atmosphere in which people don't mind taking the risk of making fools of themselves, because they know they are with friends they can trust. It may take two or three workshops before this atmosphere emerges.

LENGTH OF TIME

Each workshop will take about an hour, as already mentioned above, if you are to do it properly. Don't fall into the trap of rushing it and bombarding them with just too many ideas to absorb at one time. Remember that songs, announcements, refreshments and other bits and pieces all add to the length of things too. Keep it all moving along and use your time wisely.

FINALLY

I hope you will find this course so rewarding that you use it again and again. (Well, you didn't spend this much on a book only to use it once, did you?) I have been teaching people personal evangelism for nearly fifteen years now, and I find it one of the most exciting, satisfying things I do. It can be costly, too—you should never exhort your trainees to do anything you're unwilling to do yourself—but I don't think I've ever taught a course without learning something new from the reactions and insights of the various group members. And few things are more fulfilling than watching timid, nervous, tongue-tied Christians slowly being released into effective, articulate sharing of faith with the people they know. You can make it happen. The Apostle Paul talked about 'reliable men who will also be qualified to teach others'. And that's you! What a fabulous responsibility to have.

Go to it!

WORKSHOP 1

Evangelism—Doing What Comes Naturally

| AIM OF SESSION |

(1) To present evangelism as something *natural* and *normal*
(2) To demonstrate what the Bible actually asks us to do
(3) To confront the dread of witnessing which many Christians feel

| OUTLINE OF SESSION |

OPENING EXERCISE
|
'Evangelism is natural'
|
EXERCISE 1
|
'What a "witness" is'
|
EXERCISE 2
|
'What a "witness" needs'
|
EXERCISE 3 (optional, if time allows)

For this session you may need the following

Blank paper and pens (some of your group are sure to forget)

Copies of the questions used in the *opening exercise* (you could either have a copy for everyone, or simply write them up on a blackboard or overhead transparency)

Copies of the self-check test in EXERCISE 1

Copies of the reaction sheets in EXERCISE 3

(Plus, of course, the visuals you will be using, a copy of the relevant pages from the course notebook for everyone, and your copy of this book. These are things you will need every time—so we won't be mentioning them again.)

EXPLANATION OF CONTENT

(1) *Evangelism is natural*

After your group has completed the OPENING EXERCISE (which we'll describe later), they will have expressed some of their feelings, anticipations and fears of what is about to happen to them. Discuss with them for a few moments why we often feel apprehensive. Stress that this is a very common phenomenon; perhaps you could talk honestly about your own experiences of fright and panic.

Then get them to look at the student notebook. The answer to the question at the top of the page is: 'There must be. Otherwise, how did the church grow?' We know that natural one-to-one sharing of faith led to the great increase in the church in the early days (Acts 8:4). What we need to do is to rediscover the uncomplicated, unembarrassed style of witness of the early believers, so that witnessing becomes almost as natural as breathing.

See if your group can suggest answers to the three questions beginning 'Why?'. They should arrive at conclusions like these:

—There are few New Testament verses urging us to evangelize because the New Testament assumes that Christians will do it anyway, without needing to be told.

—There are no blow-by-blow accounts because there is no

one method especially approved by God, and guaranteed to succeed. There can be as many different methods as there are kinds of people. Jesus changed his approach constantly to suit the kind of person he was communicating with (the rich young ruler, the woman at the well, Simon the Pharisee, etc.)

—*Evangelists* are specially gifted people who enjoy evangelism and have a special aptitude for it. It is the part of Christian work they are best suited for; they are specialized people; not every Christian is an evangelist. But we are all *witnesses*, without any exceptions. To be a witness isn't a special gift, but a role we will be called on to perform again and again (Acts 1:8, I Peter 3:15). We'll say more about the difference after EXERCISE 1, but first ask your group: in a law court, what is a witness's job? The answer: to tell others *what he has seen and heard*. It isn't his job to run the trial—just to speak when called upon to do so.

Point out that this should take much of the fear out of 'witnessing'. We don't have to be clever, cultured or articulate—just willing to say what has happened to us.

Then do EXERCISE 1 with them.

(2) *What a 'witness' is*

The diagram in the notebook puts one New Testament verse into visual form—Ephesians 4:10–12, which discusses the way specially gifted people are supposed to operate in the Church. The job of evangelists, pastors, teachers, etc., is to 'equip the body' so that the *body* (in other words, all the Christians together) can do 'the work of service'. (Note: the Greek word for 'equip' was the word a fisherman would use for mending his nets to make them efficient and serviceable.)

What does this mean for us? Only some Christians are evangelists, but they can equip all the others to *witness*. Only some are teachers, but they can train the others to *disciple* those converted through witnessing, and help them grow in their new faith. Only some are pastors, but they can prepare all the others to *encourage* one another in the process of following Jesus.

EXERCISE 2 should follow quite naturally at this point . . .

(3) *What a 'witness' needs*

Let's pursue this idea of 'being a witness' a bit further. What are the three things a witness must have, in a law case, if he is to be of any use?

—A STORY TO TELL. He is useless unless he knows some basic facts. In Christian witness, there are three vital things we have to know about, and we will study them all in turn later on in the course:

(a) How to give an EXPLANATION of the facts of the Christian message (this is coming up in session 3);

(b) The EVIDENCE which supports everything you say (this is the subject of sessions 4 and 5);

(c) Ways of presenting our own EXPERIENCE of Jesus (discussed in session 6).

—A JURY TO LISTEN. R. L. Stevenson's novel *Catriona* is about a man who wants desperately to testify in a murder trial, but finds that for political reasons nobody wants to listen to his story. Many Christians are useless in evangelism because they do not have any real friends who are not Christians. It could be good to get the group to write down the names of the people they see most often from day to day, and work out how many are non-Christians. They they should put ticks by each non-Christian name—one tick for 'just an acquaintance', two for 'a friend', three for 'a really close friend'. Share the results.

They might want to think over ways in which they could deepen their relationship with some of the people listed. For example, we can deepen relationships by:

(a) doing things for the other person

(b) letting the other person do things for us (see John ch. 4)

(c) spending more time with the other person

(d) asking the other person questions about himself

(e) giving a social invitation to the other person . . . and so on.

Some of your group may even find it hard to name one single non-Christian friend. Explain that this easily happens as people move more and more into a Christian lifestyle. Old patterns of friendship die away, since so much of your time is spent with other believers in new kinds of activity, and gradually you lose contact with the non-Christian world.

Hence it's vital to work against this tendency deliberately. Encourage those group members who are in such a position to start thinking of ways in which they can begin to meet and make friends of non-Christians.

Stress that it must be genuine friendship, not scalp-hunting. A young American girl once asked a Youth for Christ worker: 'If I reject your Jesus, will you still be my friend?' That's quite a challenge!

—A REPUTATION FOR HONESTY. A witness can have a fascinating tale to tell to a packed courtroom—and still not make an impression, because he is distrusted as a liar. If your character is dubious, you won't be listened to. So we have to *be ourselves*—not adopt a false manner, or ape our personal spiritual hero, or become giggly and facetious through embarrassment. We need to *realise the strength of weakness*— courage is not the absence of fear, but the grit to keep going even when terrified. It is actually more impressive than a false, glib front; people may see our timidity, but will think, 'Well, if he's *that* scared, and still wants to tell me about it, it must be really important to him . . .' And we should *understand why we are scared*: there can be factors in our personality or background which make it naturally difficult for us—so we shouldn't feel guilty about our fears, but seek to understand them, and ask God to help us conquer them.

To sum it up, we need to be like Jesus. The final diagram expresses what he was like, and what we need to be like: totally *identified* with people (understanding them, loving them, standing alongside them) yet deeply *different* from them in the life we live. Ask the group: what will happen if we are *identified* but not *different*? (No-one will be impressed by our faith.) And if we are *different* but not *identified*? (People may shy away from us, thinking us peculiar or secretive or pompous.)

EXERCISE 3 should follow if times allows. Or close with a time of prayer together.

EXERCISES

OPENING EXERCISE Get the group to write down their

answers to these three questions, and then share their answers with one another:

'What is the biggest HOPE I have for this course—what do I hope it will do for me?'

'What is my biggest FEAR as I come to take this course?'

'What is my biggest PROBLEM in sharing my faith with others?'

You may want to have them think about the questions, and hand in written answers to them, before the session—so that you can read out anonymous answers, and make a few comments about them without embarrassing anyone. It depends on how confident group members feel in opening themselves up to one another right at the start!

EXERCISE 1 Groups who do not know one another may find it good to split into groups of two, and give each person two minutes to ask his partner questions about himself. He then has to report back to the large group, and introduce his partner to them, using the information he has learned. This exercise gives good training in listening closely to what someone else is telling you—something none of us do naturally;

OR give each person a piece of paper containing this self-check test to fill in. They should write after each statement a number from 0 to 5, depending on how strongly they agree or disagree with the statement (5 is 'I agree very strongly indeed', 3 is 'I'm quite undecided about this', 0 is 'I disagree completely'). Then get them to think for a moment about the question: What do your answers tell you about your strengths and weaknesses as a witness? In groups of two (or in one large group) encourage each person to share just one of his answers and say what it tells him about his ability to witness. Perhaps you could then pray for one another. Here is the self-check test:

'1. I find it easy to talk to strangers.

2. I sometimes find I have nothing at all to say to a person I'm with.

3. I have a large number of very good friends.

4. I find it hard to gain confidence in relationships with people.

5. I feel quite satisfied with the state of my Bible knowledge.
6. I tend to go along with what others want of me.
7. I have a natural curiosity about other people.
8. I don't think I like myself very much.'

OR in groups of two, get each person to choose a colour, then argue with his partner (using any arguments he likes) to try to convince him that his chosen colour is better than his partner's. You will find that in the process of arguing, the two people become more and more convinced they are right! It teaches a lesson about what happens when people get into an argument!

EXERCISE 2 In groups of two, discuss:
　'What worries me most about having to share my faith'
　OR 'The one thing I'd most like to change about myself is . . .'
　OR 'Which people do we know who are naturally gifted as evangelists?'

EXERCISE 3 (optional) In groups of 5–6, select one person to begin talking for a minute on a certain subject. When he is finished, he points at someone else, who must continue—but first must sum up everything the first speaker said. Then a third speaker is pointed out—and he must begin by summing up everything said by *both* previous speakers. And so on. This is a very exhausting exercise, as it forces people to listen closely to everything that is said. It demonstrates how hard we find it really to listen to other people.

OR discuss in small groups: 'What characteristic of Jesus' relationships with people do you most admire?' Give each group three minutes to decide on just one answer. Then share your results—and perhaps discuss them.

OR issue 'reaction sheets' for members to fill in anonymously and leave behind after the session. You could use a wording like this:

'As a result of this session I:
* —feel less scared about witnessing
　　　　　　　　YES　　NO　　MAYBE

* —understand better what my role in evangelism is
                    YES   NO   MAYBE
* —have seen some changes I'll need to make if I'm to be
effective
                    YES   NO   MAYBE.'

The results should help you assess whether you have accomplished your aims or not.

VISUALS

The four diagrams reproduced in the course notebook, pages 1 and 2.

BACK UP MATERIAL AND FURTHER READING

Good books on *spiritual gifts* are Peter Wagner, *Your Spiritual Gifts Can Help Your Church Grow* (Gospel Light) and Michael Green, *I Believe in the Holy Spirit* (Hodder). You'll gain a lot of ideas about *evangelism in the early church* from Michael Green's *Evangelism Now and Then* (Hodder). On *God's answers to worries and fears* in evangelism, try Rebecca Manley Pippert's *Out of the Saltshaker* (IVP), a very funny and rewarding book on the whole subject of this course, or Leroy Eims' *Winning Ways* (Victor). Jim Petersen's two books *Evangelism as a Lifestyle* and *Evangelism for Our Generation* (Navpress) are very helpful introductions to what's involved in being a witness in today's secularized society. Don't try to read them all. Just find the one which will be most helpful in adding bits to what you know already, and use it to help you prepare for the session. Any good Christian bookshop can supply these titles.

HOMEWORK

Before next session, ask members to do two things:

(a) review all the notes they have taken this time, and make sure they understand them;

(b) ask God to help them choose three non-Christian friends or acquaintances to concentrate their prayers upon. They should have the names ready when they come next time.

WORKSHOP 2

The Secret Ingredient in Evangelism

AIM OF SESSION

(1) To give a clear understanding of the importance of *prayer* in evangelism
(2) To get group members praying for their friends

OUTLINE OF SESSION

INTRODUCTORY EXERCISE
|
'Why don't we pray more?'
|
EXERCISE 1
|
'Get the right perspective about prayer'
|
'Focus your prayers with information'
|
EXERCISE 2
|
'Do's and Don'ts'
|
PRAYER TOGETHER (as much as time allows)

Rescue Shop

EXTRA PREPARATION TO DO

Make a number of forms to fill in—three for each member of the group—containing the grid in the course notebook in the section 'Focus your prayers with information'.

EXPLANATION OF CONTENT

First do the INTRODUCTORY EXERCISE

(1) *Why don't we pray more?*

The opening exercise will get the group thinking about how much time we *don't* spend in prayer—for all the importance we attach to it in theory. Why do we have problems?

To understand that, we need to look at what actually happens when we pray. The diagram in the course notebook illustrates the process. We make our requests known to God; God hears; God works on the situation in answer to prayer; the result brings a change in *us*, too, because when we see our prayers answered our faith will grow, and then we are more able and eager to pray than we were before. So then the circle begins again . . .

That means there are four major elements in the process: OURSELVES, OUR PRAYERS, GOD, and GOD'S ANSWER. And we can have problems, related to any of these points on the circle, which keep us from praying as much as we should. We can have a problem with OURSELVES (we don't feel spiritual enough for God to listen to us, so we don't bother praying much). We can have a problem with THE TIME SPENT IN PRAYER (it seems too passive, we'd rather be doing something useful). We can have a problem with GOD (we may not really believe, deep down, that he will answer). And we can have a problem with GOD'S ANSWER (answered prayer tends to bring about changes in the life of the person who prayed the prayer, and most of us do not want our peaceful lives disturbed by God). How do we change things?

At this point do EXERCISE 1, which will make group members look hard at where the problems lie in their own lives . . .

(2) *Get the right perspective about prayer*

The first important step in correcting our attitude is to realise what prayer *isn't*. **It's not just a shopping list**. Prayer is talking to a Father—'a divinely-given means of developing a relationship, not a man-made scheme for delivering requests' (John Blanchard). It can also include praise, worship, confession and thanks. How well balanced are our prayer times?

It's not a way of twisting God's arm so that he is forced to give us something he doesn't want to give. He really does want to answer our prayers (Matt. 7:7,8). But persistence is needed for two reasons:

(a) sometimes we are praying for the wrong thing, and as we continue God gently changes our mind and shows us what we *should* be praying for;

(b) there are evil spiritual forces trying to prevent us from succeeding in prayer. Prayer is spiritual warfare—hard work!

It's not a super-holy feeling. We may not feel anything special most of the time when we pray. God doesn't promise any warm glow or odd sensations. Indeed, sometimes we achieve most when we don't feel like praying at all! Jesus' story in Luke 18:1–8 has some important ideas on this point.

It's not a way of earning rewards. God doesn't answer because we have put in a certain number of hours of intercession. In fact Matthew 6:7–9 suggests the opposite. When God answers, it is because of his free grace and love—*not* because we deserve it.

Once we have clearly understood all this, the next step is . . .

(3) *Focus your prayers with information*

You can't pray properly for people unless you know something about them. How well do your group members know the three target people for whom they wish to pray especially? Get them to fill in a profile, like that at the top of page N5 in the notebook for each of their three names. They may not be able to fill in all the names there and then; they may wish to go away and think about some of the details. But as they mull over these facts about their three people, the answers should suggest lots of points about which they could pray for the people concerned.

The key to praying in depth is to use our imagination. God can use it to open up our thinking about the person concerned, and show us how best to direct our prayers. He can also use it to build our faith, and help us pray believingly for greater and greater things. So the more *specific* and *detailed* our prayer information becomes, the more fruitful our prayers can be.

EXERCISE 2 will help your group apply all this to themselves.

(4) *Do's and dont's*

This final section adds some practical ideas to make your group's prayers more effective. It can be boring just going through nine items, one after another, so it might be good to ask more experienced members of the group to be prepared to talk about one point each; or else to get the group to share, in groups of two, their own experience of the problems dealt with here.

Don't dictate how God must answer—Sometimes he finds ways of saying Yes which surprise us. The story in John 4:46–54 teaches important lessons about answered prayer.

Don't pray just 'when you feel like it'—establish a regular time and place, and stick to it. God will answer when you really mean business.

Don't let your faith go stale—stimulate and challenge it constantly by feeding your mind on the promises God makes in the Bible (there are 7487 of them!).

Don't keep your prayers safe and small—pray right to the limits of your faith, for as much as you can honestly believe.

Do include praise and worship—It feeds your faith, it increases your confidence in God, it draws you closer to God's will.

Do pray 'faith-sized' prayers—don't pray for what you can't honestly believe God will do, but do let God build your faith so that you can pray for bigger and bigger things. And remember (Ephesians 3:20) that God will often give us more than we dare to ask for!

Do pray that God will change your heart—when he starts giving you an increased sense of love and concern for other people, it will motivate you to pray much more effectively than a sense of stern duty and discipline.

Do pray continually (I Thess. 5:17)—don't save it all for your regular times of prayer, but cultivate the habit of praying as you go through the day.

Do be ready to be changed—often God needs to bring about a change *in us* before he can answer our prayers, and sometimes he will make us the answer to our own prayers (e.g.: 'Lord, why doesn't someone speak to Fred about his problems?' 'All right, my child, you do it!')

It would be silly to spend a whole session talking about prayer without actually doing any. So end the evening with a time of prayer for yourselves and all your 'target' people—in twos, in small groups, or all together.

EXERCISES

INTRODUCTORY EXERCISE: Right at the beginning, before doing anything else, get members to write down the main things they have done over the last 24 hours, in order; then get them to analyse where they spent time in prayer during that time, and how long they took in praying; then get them to work out where there might have been other chances to pray within that time, and how long for; finally get them to work out why they *didn't* pray during those times—did it just not occur to them? Or were they too engrossed in something less valuable? Or were they interrupted by family or work responsibilities? They need not share their results with one another, or with you; but the exercise should demonstrate that most of us could spend longer in prayer if we wanted, and it should also show people what their own major hindrances to prayer may be.

OR (where there is less time available) get people to write

down and share with one another a list of the major
hindrances to prayer in their own lives;

OR get people to write answers *with total honesty* to these
three questions, and then discuss the results:

> 1. Would you rather attend a prayer meeting or listen to
> a good preacher?
> 2. Could you have spent more time in prayer over the
> last three days?
> 3. If you were asked to name an answer to prayer which
> you have experienced this week, would it take you a
> while to think of one?

EXERCISE 1: Get people to share with one other person
which of the 4 reasons for not praying more is most true of
them. The two people can then pray together that God will
begin to change their attitudes;

OR have a time of open prayer during which group
members can pray through some of the ideas you've just
been discussing, and ask God to change attitudes where
necessary;

OR get members to write down individually endings to the
following two sentences:

I REALISE I DON'T PRAY MORE BECAUSE I TEND TO
FEEL THAT . . .

I WANT GOD TO CHANGE ME IN SUCH A WAY THAT
I . . .

They should then sign and date what they've written, and
keep it somewhere prominent (e.g. inside Bible or handbag)
so that they will be constantly reminded of the request made
to God.

EXERCISE 2: COMPLETING THE GRID After filling in the
profile, get group members to share the details of one of their
three friends with one other member of the group, so that
someone else can pray with them for a few minutes for this
person. (You may want these groups of 2 to get together for a
few minutes each in the remaining sessions of the course, so
that they can continue praying for the non-Christians whose
details have been shared.)

OR if you have a small group, get each member to share

details of one person, and then pray together for all the people mentioned.

OR get members to think about the three friends they have mentioned. What can they *really believe* God can do for those three people *this week*? Get them to work out a prayer request for each of the three, then to pray it throughout the next week, and be prepared to come back next week and tell the group about any answers God has given.

VISUALS

The drawing at the top of the session outline, in the course notebook, should be reproduced. Also, if members are sharing with the rest of the group some of the names of the friends they have chosen to pray for, these names and any details about them should be written on the blackboard/an OHP transparency/a big sheet of paper so that the whole group can see them and note them down. In the *Do's and Don'ts* section, it may be helpful to draw the diagram overleaf as you go along, building it up step by step.

BACK-UP MATERIAL AND FURTHER READING

You may want to read a good book about *prayer*. John White's book *People in Prayer* (IVP) is a good one (if you don't have much time, read the section on prayer in his book *The Fight* (also IVP) instead). More theologically controversial—but still very helpful on questions such as why we often feel so apathetic and why prayer can be hard work—is *Pray in the Spirit* by Arthur Wallis (Kingsway). David Watson's book *Discipleship* (Hodder) has a good brief section on prayer which crams a lot of good ideas into a small space.

Especially for younger groups, it could be valuable to have some stories of answered prayer in order to open their minds

Our prayers should be as big
as the possibilities allow —
but often they're much smaller

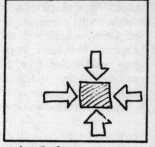

Why? Because several
forces are at work, squashing
them into insignificance...

LACK OF IMAGINATION and
LACK OF CONSISTENCY
(so: DON'T dictate how God must answer
DON'T pray just 'when you feel like it')

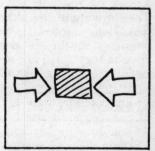

LACK OF UNDERSTANDING...
and LACK OF FAITH IN GOD
(so: DON'T let your faith go stale
DON'T keep your prayers small

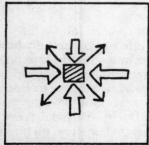

4 things we can do will exert
force in the opposite direction
(include praise + worship, pray 'faith
sized' prayers, pray that God will change
your heart, pray continually)

But the most powerful force of
all begins to operate when YOU
are ready to be changed by the
answer to your prayer

to the possibilities; good Christian biographies and real-life stories will give you many examples. (For instance, the story of George Mueller, or C. T. Studd; or from more modern times, Corrie Ten Boom or Brother Andrew. Kathleen White has written a whole series of brief lives of great Christians, published by Marshall's, which will give you some good material.)

Another idea which may be useful is the 'prayer cube' (see next page). A gimmick, yes—but anything that reminds people to pray more is worth having! A group member's watch can also be another effective reminder. Many modern digital watches have a repeating alarm function which their owners never use. Encourage owners of such watches to set them for times of the day when they want to remember to pray for their three 'targets'. Then, when the alarm goes off, they can simply switch it off, shoot up a quick prayer for their 'targets', and carry on with whatever else they were doing.

HOMEWORK

Before the next session, ask group members to read through John chapter 3 and look at the way Jesus presented his message to Nicodemus. They should notice that Jesus spoke about four subjects:

  God and his kingdom;
  What is wrong with human beings;
  Jesus' own importance;
  The response God wants from us.

All your group members have to do is to notice carefully how Jesus spoke about these things. You might want them to note down any points of interest, or questions that occurred to them, so that you can discuss it together next time; but this is not vital.

THE PRAYER CUBE

A gimmick which can help remind your group members (especially younger ones) of the need to pray!

Cut this shape out of stiff paper or cardboard, write on the sides of it as shown here (inserting the names of the three selected non-Christian friends), then fold it into the shape of a cube and stick it together.

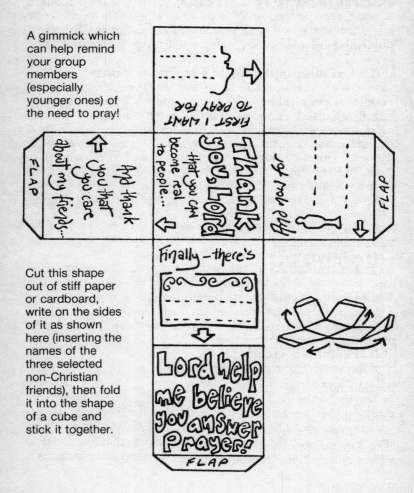

As you turn it over, looking at each side in turn, the different sides will suggest different things to pray about. Pray for some minutes about each topic before turning over to the next side.

WORKSHOP THREE

Explaining what the Good News is

AIM OF SESSION

With Nicodemus, Jesus refused to be side-tracked; he *knew what he wanted to say,* and said it. He organised his answers in *a logical order.* He *illustrated his message* with pictures—birth, wind, light—and *gave Biblical examples* to reinforce his ideas (e.g. Moses, the Holy Spirit as wind). This session aims to equip your members to:

(a) Understand the key facts of the Gospel
(b) Organise them mentally into a logical framework
(c) Illustrate them in a variety of ways
(d) Defend them from the Bible

OUTLINE OF SESSION

Introduction
|
EXERCISE 1
|
'The Key points of the Gospel'—
verses, illustrations and objections
|
EXERCISE 2
|
'Useful ways of presenting the explanation'
|
EXERCISE 3

EXTRA PREPARATION

Look through the illustrations suggested under EXERCISE 2. You may well be able to think of better ones. If so, be ready to use them during the session.

EXPLANATION OF CONTENT

(1) *Introduction*

We noticed in Session One ('A STORY TO TELL', p. 13) that presenting the Gospel involves three parts: EXPLANATION, EVIDENCE and EXPERIENCE. We are now going to learn some basic skills for communicating the first of these things— our *explanation* of the Christian message.

Get the group to think about this question. What happened between the *resurrection* and the *Great Commission*? Why didn't Jesus just send the disciples out to preach immediately after he had risen from the grave? Answer: he wanted them to have the best possible, most solid understanding of their message that they could get. So for forty days he met with them, on the greatest training course in the history of world evangelism, on a hillside in Galilee, and taught them about the kingdom of God (Acts 1:3). Without a confident grasp of our facts, our message is going to sound unconvincing.

(You could use the example of a salesman for a large company, who will have to undergo intensive training and know his product through and through before he is sent out to present it to people. Witnessing isn't quite the same thing as salesmanship—but the same principle applies!)

The word 'gospel' simply means 'good news' . . . so *any part* of the good news from God counts as part of the Gospel! That means there's a lot of it! And perhaps the only way to reproduce it fully would be to quote the whole of the Bible from start to finish. Unfortunately, not many of your friends would have the patience to sit through all that; you'd lose them well before Leviticus! And so we have to select the *most important facts* to tell people.

Get the group to decide which facts are most important (ways of doing this are suggested under EXERCISE 1, which you should do at this point). The exercise should leave you with the following list:

GOD LOVES US AND HAS GOOD INTENTIONS FOR OUR LIVES

HUMAN BEINGS HAVE LOST CONTACT WITH GOD THROUGH THEIR **WRONGDOING**

JESUS DIED TO MAKE A WAY BACK TO GOD

FORGIVENESS IS AVAILABLE THROUGH **FAITH**

Remind them that these four subjects (God, sin, Jesus, our response in faith) were the four subjects Jesus spoke of when talking to Nicodemus (last time's *Homework*). They represent the four absolutely vital facts which people need to know if they are to understand the true basis of Christian faith.

(2) *The key points of the Gospel*

Ask the group which of the four points they think should be made *first*, when talking to a non-Christian. Most will say the second one (SIN); some may say the first (GOD). It's preferable to begin with GOD because this is a positive beginning; starting with SIN doesn't sound like good news! Work out together which order is most logical and natural, and you should end up with GOD, SIN, JESUS, FAITH—then copy them into the course notebook.

(You may want to point out that each of these facts will prompt a natural question in the non-Christian's mind, to which the *next* fact gives the answer. When you talk about GOD's love, the natural question is, 'Well, if he really exists and loves me, how come I've never seen him?' So you talk about SIN and the separation it causes—which prompts the question, 'What can be done about the mess we're in, then?' The answer is that JESUS holds the answer—and so the next question is: 'How do *I* get the forgiveness I need from him?' When you then talk about FAITH, you've completed the picture.)

But it's not enough to know these facts. We need to be able to show that they are found in the Bible—we haven't just invented them; we need to be able to illustrate them meaningfully with stories and comparisons, to bring out the truth of them in a relevant way; we need to be able to anticipate objections which may be raised.

Now do EXERCISE 2.

(3) *Useful ways of presenting the explanation*

Someone once said, 'A picture is worth a thousand words'. And it has been shown that we remember much more of what we *see* than of what we merely *hear*. The BRIDGE illustration has been used for many years as a pictorial way of describing, step by step, the four key facts of the Gospel.

There is nothing sacred about this way of presenting the BRIDGE; your members may have alterations or refinements to suggest to the basic idea (though they should not allow their ideas to become too complicated!). One good idea, which saves writing it out time after time, is to draw the successive stages of the diagram on the pages of a small notebook, and flip through it page by page when explaining the Gospel to someone. Of course, the *disadvantage* of doing this is that it's a little less personal; people tend to be fascinated by a drawing which is specially created for them, but less interested in something prefabricated, no matter how nice it looks.

A different method, which allows you to back up everything you say from the Bible, is the ROMAN ROAD—a chain of verses from the Book of Romans which systematically explains the Gospel point by point. The most usual chain is shown in the course notebook (NB: in this form it starts with the fact of SIN—if you wish to begin with GOD, add in Romans 1:20 at the beginning.) Also, another chain of verses is suggested which does not rely solely on Romans, but takes in verses from several books of the New Testament. Either can be used—or more knowledgeable group members may want to work out their own version.

If group members object that they couldn't possibly remember all those references, suggest that they remember only the first one—Romans 3:23—and mark it in their Bibles. Beside it, in the margin of the Bible, they can write the reference of the next verse, so that they know where to turn

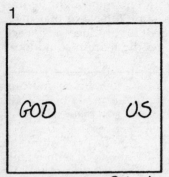

1

GOD   US

In the beginning, God and human beings were friends— with no barriers separating them

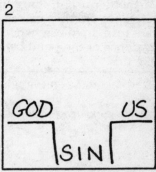

2

GOD   US
SIN

Sin brought a deep gulf into existence; God and the human race were separated by it

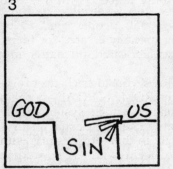

3

GOD   US
SIN

Human attempts to build bridges (being good, attending church, helping others) fail to bridge the gulf

4

GOD   US
SIN

Only Jesus' death on the cross re-established a bridge from one side to the other

to next; by the second verse they should write the reference of the third verse; and so on to the end! In this way only one verse needs to be remembered.

Another useful thing to write in the margin might be the reference of other passages on the same topic—so that they can turn to those when challenged to produce *additional* evidence of the point being made. So the margin could look like this:

```
ROMANS CHAPTER 6

Next verse:      23.  For the wages of sin
Romans 8:1            is death, but the
                      gift of God is eternal
Additional            life in Christ Jesus
verses:               our Lord.
1 Pet. 3:18,
Eph. 2:4-5
```

EXERCISE 3 gives the group some practice in trying out these techniques.

EXERCISES

EXERCISE 1: Show the 'Possible facts' visual (see below under *Visuals*) and explain that this is like many Christians' brains—crammed full of bits of isolated Bible knowledge, so that when we have to explain our faith we're not sure which bits to bring out first! Which four facts from this collection would the group select? Get them to work it out either individually or in small groups, and discuss the results.

OR: Get them to do it the other way round—deciding which facts are *less* necessary, and discarding them bit by bit until only four are left.

OR: Without showing them the 'Possible facts' visual, and without allowing them to refer to their course notebooks, ask them—in groups of two—to explain the Gospel to one another, *using only 4 facts*. Their partner will then suggest whatever he felt was left out.

EXERCISE 2: The object of this exercise is to get your group to fill in the grid given in the course notebook (obviously, they will need to draw it out again in a larger size). EITHER: in the case of a small group, fill it in together, with each member contributing suggestions:

OR: divide the group into smaller units, and give each unit an area to work on—verses, illustrations, objections (the 'illustrations' group will probably need a bit of help from you);

OR: divide into groups of two, and give each pair a fact— e.g. GOD or FAITH—to work on. Ask them to come up with a verse, an illustration and an objection in their assigned area. Then pool all the ideas.

You may find, in the case of an inexperienced group, that it takes a long time to do all this. It may be better to do a lot of it and then leave the rest for homework.

You should have your own ideas ready, in case the group can't think of a verse or illustration on any topic! Here are some suggestions for you.

GOD Verses: Acts 18:26–7, Psalm 34:8.
Illustrations: Can you believe in a God you can't see? Think of radio waves. You can't see them, but they're there all right; and you contact them whenever you switch on your radio—a receiving apparatus specially built to pick up messages from the radio waves. Man was specially built so that he could receive transmissions from the invisible God.

OR: If you are a father, you may have plans and dreams for your children. But you don't sit your child down at the age of three and tell him all your plans for his future. You guide him gently, bit by bit, as he grows to maturity. Similarly God has wonderful plans for our lives—but he will not reveal them all at once, and he will not reveal them at all if we rebel against our Father and go our own way.
Objections: You could be asked, 'Who made God, then?' Or: 'If there is a God of love, why is there so much suffering?' Or: 'Surely science has disproved the idea that God created everything?'

(Note: you don't have to *answer* these objections at this point—we'll do that in Sessions 4 and 5. All you need do for the moment is identify those most likely to arise.)

SIN Verses: Romans 3:23, Isaiah 59:1,2.

Illustrations: If a radio stops working, it _could_ be that all the radio stations in the world have mysteriously stopped transmitting. It _could_ be that there's no such thing as radio anyway, and our previous experiences of listening to it were just delusions. But it's much more likely that there's something wrong inside your appliance. Human beings are no longer receiving the transmissions God sends out—why? Because he's not there or any more? Or because he's just a delusion? No; once again, there's _something wrong inside_.

_OR_: once there was an accident in a submarine while it was underwater. A panel sprang a leak, and one whole compartment filled up with water. The experts—who knew what to do, and how to control the submarine—were isolated at one end; but two visitors to the submarine, who had no idea of how it all worked, were trapped at the other end. In the same way, our lives are separated from God, the expert who made us, by a solid barrier just like the tons of water in the submarine.

Objections: 'But if I live a good life, won't that be enough?' 'Surely a God of love wouldn't condemn anybody?' 'Are you suggesting I'm a bad person, like a bank robber or a murderer?'

JESUS Verses: I Peter 3:18, John 3:16.

Illustrations: The son of a judge committed a serious crime, and was taken to court as a result. His father judged the case, and imposed a very large fine upon his son. Then he stepped down from his chair, pulled some money from his pocket, and paid the fine himself. That was the meaning of the death of Jesus: God passing sentence upon us, and then meeting the demands of the law himself by sending his Son to die.

_OR_: in the Warsaw Ghetto in the Second World War, Jews were cut off from the outside world by walls—just as sin cuts us off from God. One man, called Mietek, risked death by travelling outside the ghetto walls every night to buy bread and meat for the ghetto. He became the living link between one side and the other—by putting his own life in danger. Jesus became the link between God's side and ours, not by risking his life, but by surrendering it completely.

Objections: 'But wasn't Jesus just a good man?' 'Is Jesus the only way—what about other religions?' 'What sort of cruel God allows His Son to suffer like that?'

FAITH Verses: Romans 10:9, Ephesians 2:8,9.
Illustrations: You are walking across a field in winter. Suddenly you come to a frozen pond. To walk round it would take hours, but you're not sure the ice would take your weight. You look at it but can't decide if it's thick enough. How do you find out? There's only one way: try it for yourself.

OR: It's like getting married. You make promises to the other person, believing that he/she loves you and wants to keep the promises he/she is also making. You could be wrong! You could have a terrible marriage and be let down completely! But you commit yourself because you are prepared to trust the other person.

Objections: 'But how will I know it's real?' 'Surely you have to do *something* about it.' 'Isn't it all just a figment of your imagination, psychological conditioning?'

EXERCISE 3: Divide the group into pairs, and get them to take turns at presenting the Gospel to one another, as if the other person were a non-Christian. The first time, the presenter of the Gospel should use the Bridge; the next time, the Roman Road should be used. It doesn't matter if the group members are too unfamiliar with these new ideas to be able to do it very well. It's the practice that counts.

OR: Divide the group into two teams. Each team takes it in turns to challenge one individual from the other side to quote a verse, illustration or objection connected to one of the four points. (For example: 'Give me a *verse* about *sin*.') If he can name one within fifteen seconds, his side scores a point; if he can't, the challengers score a point.

OR: Get the members to divide into groups of four, then get each group to present the Gospel to you, point by point. To start the group off, point at one member, who must explain the first fact (GOD) to you; then to another member, who must explain the second fact (SIN); and so on.

VISUALS

The most central visual diagram of the whole course is this one:

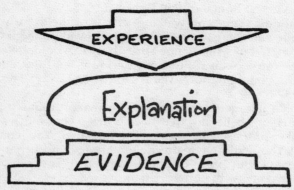

It could be good to make a big, permanent copy of it, which you could refer to during the next few sessions too.

The 'POSSIBLE FACTS' visual, used in Exercise 1, is:

Remember, too, that you will need to draw the BRIDGE diagram, step by step, in front of the group. Practise and become familiar with it.

BACK-UP MATERIAL AND FURTHER READING

A good book on simple *Christian teaching* could help to refresh your memory of the basics of the faith. For instance, Peter Cotterell's *This is Christianity* (IVP) or *Let the Bible Teach You Christian Doctrine* (Paternoster) by J. J. Davis. Many of the best *evangelistic paperbacks* contain illustrations and stories which you could use instead of those suggested in this chapter: look at Michael Green's *You must be Joking* (Hodder), David Day's *This Jesus* (IVP), or John Young's *The Case Against Christ* (Kingsway).

Some of the best books on *personal evangelism* give a clear explanation of how to explain the basic facts of the Gospel. Paul Little's classic *How to Give Away your Faith* (IVP) and Ross Pilkinton's *How to Evangelize the Jesus Way* (SU) may be very useful here.

Many of the best-known evangelistic leaflets which you will find in Christian bookshops—'Four things God wants you to know', 'Have you heard of the Four Spiritual Laws?', 'The Little Green Book'—are based on the same four-facts approach to the Gospel as is explained in this session. It could be worthwhile taking a few copies along with you, to demonstrate that this really is an effective and logical way of putting the basis of the message across to people.

HOMEWORK

If group members have not completed the grid during the session, get them to do it at home. If they *have*, get them to study it throughout the week until they can remember most of it quite clearly. And get everyone to ask three non-Christians to tell them why they find it difficult to believe what Christians say about God.

WORKSHOP 4

Producing Evidence
For What You Say

AIM OF SESSION

And also of the following one:

(1) To give group members enough evidence to produce good answers to objections which might be made to them
(2) To make these answers crisp and confident enough not to waste time
(3) To make these answers gracious enough not to offend
(4) (Perhaps, if time allows) to produce the skill of shifting from the defensive (answering questions) to the offensive (challenging the questioner personally)

OUTLINE OF SESSION

Introduction
|
'How can you believe in someone you can't see?'
|
'Who made God?'
|
EXERCISE 1
|
'Would a God of love allow suffering?'
|
'Why the Christian God?'
|
EXERCISE 2

41

EXPLANATION OF CONTENT

(1) *Introduction*

The biggest worries about personal evangelism are usually based on fears of the objections that might be raised. 'What if he asks me some question I've no idea about? I'll look stupid!' It is important to stress to group members that most people ask the same few questions as everybody else. There are only a very few basic ones, and the twelve we shall be covering will answer most situations. And in the next session we shall give some guidelines for dealing with completely original questions too!

Find out how the group got on with the homework exercise. Which were the most common objections they heard? You'll probably find that most of them boil down to just four questions—the ones we'll be looking at in this session.

So let's examine some answers to the first of them . . .

(2) *How can you believe in someone you can't see?*

SOMETIMES WE HAVE TO: It makes sense to believe in electricity, although we've never seen it; and to believe in Uncle George in Toronto, though we've never seen him either. Why? We know they're there because we *see the effects* (electricity makes lights and heaters work; Uncle George sends us birthday presents.) In the same way, the Bible claims that anyone willing to experience God will soon see the effects in his life.

IF YOU *COULD* SEE HIM, WOULD YOU BELIEVE?: Suppose God suddenly appeared in front of you. You'd probably think it was an illusion or a hallucination; and even if you were temporarily convinced, later you wouldn't be quite sure. It would be too unlike your normal experiences to carry conviction. Much better if God could stay invisible, yet provide so many proofs of his involvement with you that you were left in no doubt.

HOW DO PEOPLE MAKE RELATIONSHIPS?: Friendships are built, not upon sight (or a blind person could never make any friends!), but upon communication; I do things with you, you do things with me, and we exchange ideas. All of this, the Bible says, is possible in a relationship with God.

(3) *Who made God?*

The implication behind this questions is that nothing 'just happened'—everything had to be made by something else. If so, what *started* the whole process? You could say 'Nothing—it's just gone on that way for ever'. But you would be making a statement of blind faith with no evidence behind it whatsoever. There is no way of finding out the truth of the statement; whereas *if* God exists, he *can* be verified. Or you could say, 'Something *did* begin the process'. Now that could as easily be *God*, as some kind of blind force. If God exists, he is by definition the ultimate; so to suggest that something may have existed before him, and made him, is nonsensical. If there was something else first, he isn't God—by definition!

Now break to do Exercise 1.

(4) *Would a God of love allow suffering?*

This question is often the most sensitive and personal one which can be asked. Few of us go through life without encountering our share of personal tragedy, and often someone asking this question will have hurtful past experiences in mind. So answers need to be especially careful, thoughtful and gentle.

GOD DOESN'T LIKE IT EITHER: God is not someone who enjoys inflicting pain, or is indifferent to it. He cares and grieves more than we do about a world in a mess. It hurts him—because he made it and planned it to be very different. It is important right at the start to give the questioner a correct picture of God's attitude to suffering.

FREE WILL CAN BE MISUSED: The real problem is that when God made man he gave us freedom to choose our own course—without it we would have been merely robots or puppets—and we chose to use it wrongly. We have turned our backs on God and allowed evil to rule our lives. Consequently we, and other people, get hurt. Most trouble in the world is caused by human evil.

RULES MUST BE KEPT: God has made the universe in such a way that it operates on certain fixed principles—the sun always rises in the east, rain always falls downwards rather than upwards, water always freezes at a certain temperature. If he changed those rules from moment to moment, life would not only be unpredictable, it would be impossibly dangerous. And so when people do something which brings them into conflict with the laws of nature (e.g. smoking and damaging their lungs) God will not suspend those laws for five minutes to keep them from harm. The laws stay in operation; if we choose to harm ourselves, God will not prevent us.

CREATION HAS BEEN SHATTERED: The Bible claims (Genesis 3:14–19) that in some way human sin shattered the mainspring of creation. *Nothing* works the way it should any more—which is why volcanoes, earthquakes and droughts threaten human life and bring undeserved tragedy. Now we can't prove that this is how the world became such a confusing mixture of good and evil, but it makes at least as much sense as the other possibilities (i.e. that there is no God,—in which case it's hard to explain the order and design in creation—or that there's a God of hate and evil—in which case it's hard to explain the existence of beauty and happiness).

(5) *Why the Christian God?*

'Don't all religions lead to God?' The idea that different religions are just alternative paths up the side of a hill, and that all will meet at the top when they reach God at the summit, is attractive but misleading. Not many hills are perfectly rounded, and sometimes hill paths wander all over the place! Not all routes lead to the top; some go round in circles, and others end on the brink of a precipice. Similarly some beliefs go round in circles, and others lead to disaster.

If all religions lead to God, (a) none can be much use, since the data they give is totally contradictory; (b) God can't care much about us, or he'd have given us a clear revelation rather than letting us disagree about everything; (c) Christianity must be untrue, as it claims to be the only way to God (John 14:6, Acts 4:12).

Eastern religions believe in a God who is a tremendous, transcendent force (symbolised by the cloud on the diagram at the foot of the page in the course notebook) but who is not necessarily a person with real thoughts and feelings. Western gods tend to be extremely human and personal (the gods of the Romans and the Norsemen, for example) but not to be very powerful or holy. Only in Christianity do we find a God both personal *and* transcendent, capable of satisfying the desires of East and West.

EXERCISES

EXERCISE 1: In groups of two, practise answering these first two questions. Stop the other person when he says something hard to understand, or contradictory. (NB: It is not essential that your group members should stick rigidly to the answers supplied in this book. They may have extra arguments and ideas which they want to use as well; that's fine, as long as the ideas are logical! But they should use *some* of the session material as well.)

OR: Select three people to answer the same question in front of the group. Decide amongst yourselves which answer was best, and why.

OR: Explain the importance of being able to switch from the defensive to the offensive—from simply answering objections, to positively presenting the Christian challenge. (See *Aim of session* (4) above). Get the group members, in small groups, to work out ways of answering the questions and then switching on to the offensive (e.g., with 'Who Made God':' . . . So if you believe everything's always been the way it is, you're placing your faith in something you can't prove. And if you believe some blind force began everything, you're placing your faith in something you can't prove. But God *can* be verified. Are you willing to put him to the test?').

EXERCISE 2: In groups of about six, one person is chosen to

answer one of the four questions. Having done so, he
chooses another person at random and gives him a different
question to answer. This person then does the same. The
process continues as long as you wish.

OR: In pairs, take turns at explaining some of the points
given in answer to the questions 'Would a God of love allow
suffering?' and 'Why the Christian God?' Stop the other
person when anything is said which is hard to understand, or
contradictory.

OR: If some of your group members are intelligent and
experienced enough, use them to act the part of 'Devil's
Advocate'. Assign each of them to a small group of others,
and ask them to raise the kind of objections with the group
which a non-Christian might raise when discussing these
four questions. This should give your group members
experience in not only answering the questions, but also
countering other points which might be raised.

VISUALS

The diagrams in the course notebook could be used. Here is
an additional suggestion for the question 'Would a God of
love allow suffering?' (see diagram opposite).

BACK-UP MATERIAL
AND FURTHER READING

There are several books of *evidence for Christianity* which will
be very useful to you both in this session and in the next.
John Allan and Gus Eyre have written *Express Checkout*
(Paternoster), which gives crisp factual answers to eighty of
the most common objections raised by non-Christians; and
there's a whole section on 'Questions about God'. *It Makes
Sense* by Stephen Gaukroger (SU) begins with a section on
'Can I believe in God?' If you don't have much time, John

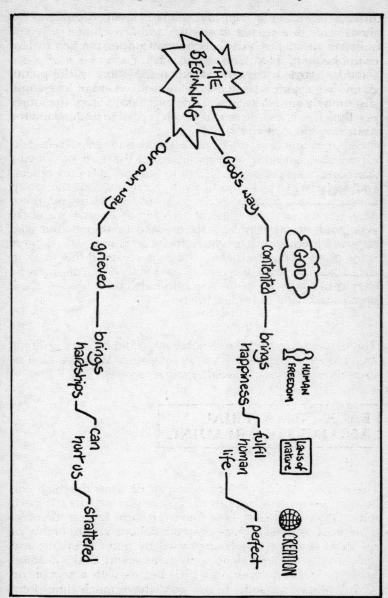

Allan's *Sure Thing* (Kingsway) is a brief, snappy guide to the main kinds of evidence we have.

Books about *God* and the Christian understanding of him might be helpful too. The classic is J. I. Packer's *Knowing God* (Hodder), which contains some really solid teaching, but don't be frightened—it is written in a very engaging, disarmingly simple style which makes it very easy to absorb. For those with less time, *God* by Steve Brady (SU) covers the basic facts quickly and simply.

HOMEWORK

Ask your group members to go back to the friends who supplied them with a list of objections last time, and ask them if they can try out on them the answers learned this week. It could lead to some interesting conversations! Alternatively they could go back to the same friends and interview them about their view of Jesus Christ.

WORKSHOP 5

Arguments and Evidence

AIM OF SESSION

See Aim of Session 4.

OUTLINE OF SESSION

'Was he what the Bible claims?'
|
'Is the data trustworthy?'
|
'Did he rise from the grave?'
|
'Was he just a good man?'
|
EXERCISE 1
|
'Won't a good life do?'
|
'Isn't it all about imagination?'
|
'What about those who haven't heard?'
|
'Hasn't science disproved it all?'
|

EXERCISE 2
|
'Questions you can't answer'
|
'Finally, remember . . .'
|
EXERCISE 3 (OPTIONAL)

EXTRA PREPARATION

Memorise the main facts of the resurrection story so that you
can tell it to the group in a connected way. If using the 'circle
of knowledge' game in EXERCISE 2, make up one set of the
necessary cards for every five people in your group. Or if
using a different option on EXERCISE 2, you might need to
make up some 'fallacious arguments'.

EXPLANATION OF CONTENT

Not all the questions most commonly asked are about God.
Many are about Jesus, and others about Christian experience.
And so this week we're going to examine four questions
about JESUS, then four about CHRISTIAN EXPERIENCE.
Begin the session by finding out how the homework exercise
went. Did anybody have an interesting encounter? What are
the main ideas non-Christians have about Jesus? Let's look
closely at four of the major objections.

(1) *Was He what the Bible claims?*

Here are three good reasons for believing he was.

   CONFIRMATION BY OTHER WRITERS: Non-Christian
authors confirm details of Jesus' life. Flavius Josephus, the
greatest Jewish historian, wrote this just 60 years after Jesus'
death:

At this time there was a wise man who was called Jesus. And his conduct was good and he was known to be virtuous. And many people from among the Jews and from the other nations became his disciples. Pilate condemned him to be crucified and to die. And those who had become his disciples did not abandon his discipleship. They reported that he had appeared to them three days after his crucifixion and that he was alive. Accordingly he was perhaps the Messiah . . .

Tacitus, the eminent Roman historian, wrote twenty years later:

Christus was executed at the hand of the procurator Pontius Pilate in the reign of Tiberius. Although checked for the moment, this pernicious superstition (of Christianity) broke out, not only in Judea, the source of the evil, but even in Rome . . .

These are just the best two of many quotations one could cite.

VERY EARLY MANUSCRIPTS: We have texts for the New Testament which go back to just a few decades after Jesus lived. We know the earliest Gospel may well have been written within 20 years of Jesus' death. If the stories about him were just wild legends, it would have been impossible to circulate them in areas where the true facts were well known, just 20 years after the event!

ARCHAEOLOGICAL EVIDENCE: We can be confident that the early Christians believed right from the start in Jesus as the Son of God. The word square in the course notebook was a pattern which Christians used to inscribe on the walls of their houses. When the letters were rearranged, it spelled:

```
            A
            P
            A
            T
            E
            R
A  P A T E R N O S T E R  O
            O
            S
            T
            E
            R

            O
```

—the Latin words for 'Our Father' in the shape of a cross, surrounded by the letters A and O (Alpha and Omega). It meant: the man who died was the same as 'Our Father'— truly God—and the Alpha and Omega, the beginning and the end. There are many other archaeological finds which demonstrate the early Christians' belief in Jesus' divinity.

(2) *Is the data trustworthy?*

Again, three good reasons!

RELIABLE TEXT: We have more, and better, texts of the New Testament than of any other book of the period. The text of Caesar's *Gallic Wars*, for example, is based on just one ninth-century copy of a manuscript; for the New Testament we have about 4500 complete manuscripts, lots of fragments, and scores of thousands of quotations in other works of the time. We're not in any real doubt about what the original text said!

NOBODY COULD INVENT SUCH A CHARACTER: Jesus' teaching was unique, profound, the greatest in Jewish history for several hundred years. Anyone who invented such a fictional character would be a genius himself. None of the early Christian writers were like that.

INCIDENTAL DETAILS PROVE TO BE CORRECT: All sorts of historical facts mentioned in the Bible have been queried, but found accurate. The Gospel writers were very careful and scrupulous; Luke, for instance, talks about fifteen different titles for Roman governors and uses the right one on every single occasion. It used to be thought that Pontius Pilate never existed, that the Gospels had invented him; but then a slab was dug up at Caesarea containing the name of Pilate *and* that of the Emperor Tiberius—thus neatly proving, both that he lived, and also *when* he lived. The 'Pavement' mentioned in John's Gospel was held to be fictional, until 2500 square metres of it were excavated in north-west Jerusalem . . . and so on. The Gospels contain factual data, not imaginative fiction.

(3) *Did he rise from the grave?*

The most effective way of working on this question may be to point out to the group the three possible alternative explanations of what might have happened if Jesus *hadn't* risen again; then to tell the story listing the facts we're sure of, while group members listen for important details to show them why none of these alternative theories are possible. (The three theories are listed in the student notebook).

The story would go something like this:

'Jesus died by crucifixion, and a crucified man could prolong his life for a while by pushing down against the nails in his feet, to relieve the strain on his chest. The religious leaders didn't want this to happen, as they wanted Jesus dead before the Feast of the Passover, due to begin that evening. During Passover no Jew would touch a dead body, so there would be problems in disposal.

'So soldiers came round to smash the legs of the victims with a mallet. They saw Jesus had died so did something different: they stuck a spear into his side, at which there came out a trickle of what looked like blood and water. They then notified the governor that Jesus had died. He then ordered a double check, and the Jews insisted on the tomb being guarded.

'Jesus' body was prepared for burial, tied in bandages with a heavy weight of spices piled on the body, and placed in a rock tomb with a stone rolled in front—a massive stone, according to the Bible; and certainly large ones were used in those days. The tomb was sealed, i.e. a rope was stretched round the stone, and secured at either end with a blob of wax bearing the Emperor's personal stamp. To break the seal was treason against the Empire.

'A guard was placed on the tomb—either a Roman century, which would have meant 100 soldiers divided into three watches, each spending three hours on duty and six off; or the Jewish temple guard, fanatically devoted to the Jewish leadership, and sternly disciplined.

'In the middle of the third night, there was an earth tremor—common in Jerusalem—and the stone rolled away from the tomb, revealing the fact that the body was gone. The grave cloths were lying intact, but there was obviously nothing in them; the soldiers ran to consult the Jewish leaders, and a statement was issued that the soldiers had fallen asleep (an offence which should have been punished by death, but strangely wasn't). No-one seems to have believed the story, and within six weeks over 3000 Jerusalem residents had accepted the claim that Jesus was alive again. The resurrection details are mentioned as accepted fact in one of the oldest New Testament letters—I Corinthians—written just 20 years after the events.'

This account contains enough detail for your members to be able to find objections against all three alternative explanations.

(4) *Was he just a good man?*

Few people would deny his goodness, his selflessness, the value of his teaching. Yet he undeniably claimed to be God (e.g. John 5:18–27). That leaves only three possibilities. *Was he mad?* Unlikely; Jews hated madness, and had he shown any sign of instability during the 3 hard-pressured years in which he lived at close contact with the disciples, he would have been quickly abandoned. Even his enemies did not claim this of him. *Was he bad*, a trickster trying to gain power? Unlikely, as he went to his death stubbornly claiming to be God—even when it was not likely to do him any good, but would just seal his death sentence. This does not sound like the behaviour of a trickster.

That leaves just one possibility. *Maybe he was who he claimed to be* . . . (Before going on to the next group of questions, do EXERCISE 1 at this point).

(5) *Won't a good life do?*

Here are 3 points to remember:

WHAT IS 'GOOD'? Who decides? Different human beings set a different standard for 'goodness'. Surely only God has the right to decide. Yet if we look at his standards in the Bible, every human being falls short of them. You may be 99% good or 5% good, but if you don't reach God's standard of 100%, you've failed just the same.

(When talking about science, resist the urge to be side-tracked into a debate on evolution, or the possibility of extra-terrestrial life, or the feasibility of Noah's Ark. Stick to the main point—talk about principles, not specific instances, or you may become involved in a lengthy, inconclusive discussion which bogs down the whole presentation.)

(9) *Questions you can't answer* and (10) *Finally, remember . . .*

These last two sections don't need much explaining. (9) simply offers 3 points to remember when confronted with a mystifying question: admitting we don't know is not a bad thing, as when confronted with a mystifying question: admitting we don't know is not a bad thing, as it reveals our honesty; offering to find the answer shows we are open-minded; and keeping our promise gives us another chance to talk. (10) makes three important points about the *way in which* we answer questions—just as important as what we say. All the material you need is in the student notebook.

Finish with EXERCISE 3.

EXERCISES

EXERCISE 1: Test out the facts which have been absorbed by giving a short quiz, such as:

1. Name two non-Christian writers who talked about Jesus as a real person.
2. How soon after Jesus' death were the Gospels written?
3. How does the SATOR word-square show us what early Christians believed?
4. How many manuscripts of the New Testament do we possess?
5. Who guarded the tomb of Jesus?
6. Give one incidental detail from the Gospels which has been proved correct.

OR: Divide the group into two teams and give them a minute each to think of all the evidence they can in answer to one of the four questions about Jesus which we have been considering. The more facts they can name within the minute, the more marks they score.

OR: Divide into pairs and get each member to test his partner out on how much of this information he can remember.

EXERCISE 2: The 'circle of knowledge' game. Make out twelve cards containing the following inscriptions:

'1. Josephus was a Roman writer whose statements backed up Jesus' reality. True 3; False 12.'

'12. Science attempts to answer the question 'How' but the Bible talks about 'Why'. True 3, False 6.'

'3. A very early New Testament passage talks about witnesses of the Resurrection. I Cor. 15 (6); Colossians 2 (8).'

'6. There were not enough guards at the tomb of Jesus for us to be sure that they didn't all fall asleep. True 11; False 8.'

'8. There are only three possibilities about Jesus: mad, bad or God. True 11; False 9.'

'11. Jesus' wounds on the cross prove he was dead when taken down. True 9; False 4.'

'9. Some people are naturally more able to live a good life than others. True 4; False 7.'

'4. Romans 2 teaches that people who have ignored the Gospel will be given a second chance after death. True 2; False 7.'

'7. God knows how those who have never heard would have responded to the Gospel. True 2; False 10.'

'2. One reason for assurance is what happens inside you—inner changes leading to a new lifestyle. True 10; False 5.'

'10. There are many existing manuscripts of the New Testament. The number is 5400 (1) or 4500 (5).'

'5. Scientific training makes it difficult to believe in God. True 1; False 12.'

Make one set of these cards for every five people in your group. Then divide the group into fives, and get each group of five to try to place the cards in order. Each card contains a question with two possible answers; if on card 1 (for example) they think the correct answer is 'True' they should go on to card 3, and if they think the correct answer is 'False' they should go on to card 12. If they continue in this way, and get all the answers right, the cards should go round in a circle, the last one leading back to the first. The winners are the first group to complete the circle. The circle will not work unless all answers are correct.

OR: Select three group members to form a 'panel of experts' The rest of the group throw questions at them, deriving from the content of this section, and try to catch them out. If one of the experts is unable to answer a question, he leaves the panel, and the questioner takes his place.

OR: Give the group some fallacious arguments to work on. Get them to try and sort out where the flaws in the arguments are. Here's an example:

I don't believe in God. What sort of monster would allow people into heaven because they're dutiful little Christians, worshipping Jesus Christ, and send others to hell when maybe they haven't even heard about Christianity? No, I think Christians are building their lives on an illusion anyway. I mean, you can't know God's there unless you see him—and they haven't. They just have this funny feeling deep in their hearts. That doesn't prove anything; it's just wishful thinking.

EXERCISE 3: If you haven't yet given some practice to the group in going from the defensive to the offensive (see Session 4), it could be good to do so now.

OR: Divide into groups of three. One person acts the part of a belligerent non-Christian, who can be as rude as he likes; a second person acts the part of a Christian who is trying to discuss his faith graciously with him; the third person is the referee, who must ensure that the Christian is given a fair chance by the non-Christian, and must stop the exercise when he feels it has gone far enough.

OR: In groups of 2, each member asks his partner one of the twelve questions we have covered, and then awards marks for his answer in three areas: first, 0–5 for graciousness; second, 0–5 for content; and third, 0–5 for skill in switching from defensive to offensive.

VISUALS

Some which may be helpful are:

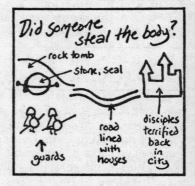

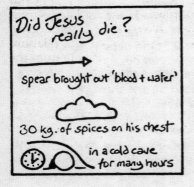

BACK-UP MATERIAL
AND FURTHER READING

There are many good books on *the evidence about Jesus*, such as Josh McDowell's *Evidence that Demands a Verdict* (Campus Crusade) and John Drane's *Jesus and the Four Gospels* (Lion). On *Christianity and science*, try Denis Alexander, *Beyond Science* (Lion) or Donald Mackay, *The Clockwork Image* (IVP). Some non-Christian writers have produced good books arguing that there is lots of evidence of planning and purpose in nature, that the world can't just have come about by chance—for instance, Gordon Rattray Taylor's *The Great Evolution Mystery* (Abacus) and Francis Hitching's *The Neck of the Giraffe; or Where Darwin Went Wrong* (Pan). Some good tapes on Christian evidence (and especially on the relationship between Christianity and science) are available from the London Institute for Contemporary Christianity, Vere St., London, W1M 9HP.

You can read more about how to present your arguments in Paul Little's book *How to Give Away Your Faith* (IVP) and *Express Checkout*, which we referred to last time. Campus Crusade have a booklet, 'Turning the Tables in Witnessing', which is the best guide available to how to switch from the defensive to the offensive in answering people's questions.

HOMEWORK

Ask your group members to talk to two other Christians (preferably not members of the group) and ask them to share their story, with full details of how and why they accepted Christ. Additionally, you could challenge your members to present some of the evidence they have gained this week to a non-Christian friend, and report back on what happens.

WORKSHOP 6

Sharing Your Experience

To enable members to tell their own story in a logical order; briefly enough to be interesting; in terms that make sense to a non-Christian; and with confidence, but also total honesty.

OUTLINE OF SESSION

Introduction: *EXERCISE 1*

'What can prevent your story from being understood?'

EXERCISE 2

'The structure of your story'

'How to learn it'

EXERCISE 3

EXTRA PREPARATION

You may wish to ask some group members to act as readers for the 'fake testimonies' (see EXERCISE 2).

EXPLANATION OF CONTENT

Use EXERCISE 1 right at the beginning to get things moving. Then continue:

(1) *What can prevent your story from being understood?*

Most of us are not trained in telling our own story. It is just assumed that we know it well enough to tell it interestingly. And the idea of practising it seems artificial; surely it will sound more natural and fresh if we do not prepare? But in fact unprepared testimonies can run into several problems: *JARGON*—sometimes we use phrases and words which make perfect sense to ourselves, because we know what the Bible says and we have heard these expressions at church many times, but which leave non-Christians perplexed; *OVER-MODESTY*—having heard so many testimonies from converted drug smugglers and murderers, we feel we don't have much of interest to say, but in fact if we can make our story sound human and credible there will be plenty of interest in it; *EXAGGERATION*—making a neater story by twisting the facts slightly, or enhancing the interest by adding in details which aren't quite true; *TOO MUCH CONTENT*—trying to get all the theological points we can into our story instead of simply telling it straightforwardly; *REPETITION*—saying the same thing several times because we haven't worked out a clear idea of what order to put things in; and *IRRELEVANCE* —dragging in details which aren't very important. Often irrelevance is caused by nerves: telling your own story is a little embarrassing, so it's easier to talk about the colour of the preacher's tie than about our own inner feelings.

Explain each of these potential mistakes, and then do EXERCISE 2. Don't worry if you haven't used up much of the session time yet; the next part will take a long time!

(2) *The structure of your story*

There are three parts to anyone's story:
  BEFORE—here the temptation is to paint one's previous

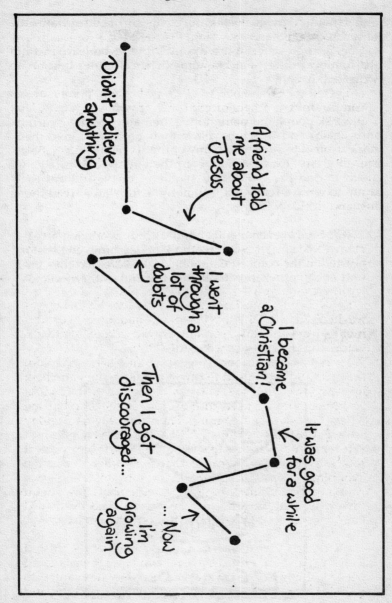

that night I trusted Jesus to come and see him afterwards. So I did and that night I trusted Jesus for the first
time. The preacher said we could, if we wanted to. So I
did. I was fifteen at the time when I trusted Jesus.
(REPETITION).

You can invent others of your own if you wish.

OR: Ask people, in pairs, to tell their story to their partner
once again, and this time allow their partner to give them
marks from 0 to 5 for how many of the six pitfalls (i.e. jargon,
over-modesty, exaggeration, etc.) they manage to avoid.

OR: Divide the group into smaller groups, and get each
group to write a really *bad* testimony. Afterwards, read them
out, and decide which is worst!

EXERCISE 3: Let each member of the group work on parts 1–3
of 'How to learn it' (the method of learning one's story
suggested in the course notebook). Make sure that they try it
out on one another in pairs before the end of the session.

VISUALS

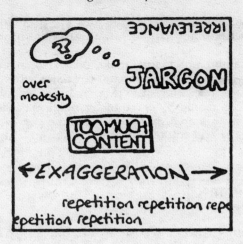

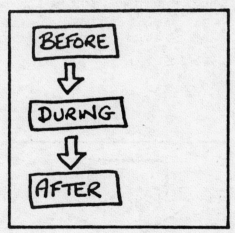

BACK-UP MATERIAL
AND FURTHER READING

Read well-told stories of testimony, such as *The Cross and the Switchblade* and other Christian paperbacks, and analyse why they are successful. What techniques are used to hold the reader's attention and convey an atmosphere of immediacy and credibility?

Unfortunately, not many books on personal evangelism seem to say much about how to tell your own story. There's a section in *Life-Style Evangelism* (Marshall) by Joseph Aldrich, called 'Your Personal Message of Evangelism'; it isn't really much help in this area, but contains some very worthwhile ideas anyway. You could find it rewarding to look at.

HOMEWORK

Ask the group to carry out parts 4 and 5 of 'How to learn it' in the student notebook; then to report next week on what happened.

WORKSHOP 7

Knowing How Much to Say, and When to Say It

AIM OF SESSION

(1) To help members understand why we often feel scared to say anything
(2) To develop sensitivity in knowing when to talk and when not to
(3) To impart the skill of beginning an embarrassment-free conversation about Jesus

OUTLINE OF SESSION

EXERCISE 1
|
'Don't let the Devil overwhelm you with false guilt'
|
'How to develop your boldness'
|
EXERCISE 2
|
'How to begin a conversation—recognizing God's time'
|
EXERCISE 3

EXPLANATION OF CONTENT

The last four sessions have given us a pretty good basis of information to present, and skills in presenting it. Yet it's possible to have all that, to be awesomely clued-up, and yet be useless in evangelism . . . through simple embarrassment. What good does it do to stuff our heads with witnessing techniques and evidence for the resurrection if it gets choked up inside and can't find a way out?

(Teaching this session demands more sensitivity to people than any of the others so far. We're all different in the way we relate to other people in the world around us. And as a result, activities which will be perfectly normal and straightforward for one person will make another want to curl up and die with shame. Jesus Christ wants his witnesses to be normal and true to the basic personality with which he created them—not a bunch of artificial robots applying someone else's patent system for machine-producing converts. So be careful that you don't talk about 'boldness' in such a way that it makes the more timid members feel they have to be brash extroverts, riding roughshod over the feelings of their in converted friends, before they can communicate Jesus. On the other hand, because people will always take the easiest option available to them, guard against implying that there is no urgency or courage required in communicating the Gospel. We *do* have to take the occasional social risk, and chance taking the initiative for Jesus. This session should simply allow people to see that (a) the responsibility of boldness exists (b) we don't have to worry about developing unnatural assertiveness or aggression, but just be prepared to let Jesus use us quite naturally in situations which *he* has prepared for us and put in front of us.)

EXERCISE 1 should bring it home to members' minds that lack of courage is a problem for *all* of us. The first thing to do is to analyse why it happens.

(1) *Don't let the Devil overwhelm you with false guilt*

The Devil can keep us going round in a frustrating circle (see diagram in student course notebook) by telling us bigger and bigger lies. Go through the examples listed in the student notebook and get the group to suggest others. Why are these examples untrue? Where is the lie?

Remember that one of the Bible's titles for the Devil is 'the Accuser'. (In fact, that's what the word means—it comes from the verb *diaballein*, which means 'to slander, to misrepresent'. One of his favourite ways of dissuading us from doing what God wants is to make us feel guilty.

(2) *How to develop your boldness*

The notebook gives six ideas, each based on a verse from the Bible: Phil. 1:14, Eccl. 11:4, Prov. 28:1, Acts 4:12, Jer. 20:9, Acts 4:29. (This list was first suggested by Leroy Eims in his useful book *Winning Ways*, which we've already mentioned.) Get the group to decide which idea links with which verse, and to discuss the meaning of each.

Now do EXERCISE 2 . . .

(3) *Recognizing God's time*

Some people respond to the Gospel the first time they hear it. That's great. But most people do not have such a straightforward reaction. It can take a long time for them to make up their mind, and in the process they will go through lots of 'mini-decisions', as Jim Petersen puts it (*Evangelism for our Generation*, Navpress, 1985). These decisions are about such things as: do I like this Christian who seems keen to be my friend? Do I want to spend time with him? Does he seem to be a freak or could there be something real about this experience of his? Do I want to accept his invitation to come to a meeting? Will I ask him some of my questions or not? How honest do I want to be? Should I read a book about this? Would it be a good idea to explore Christianity for myself? Do I care what my friends think about it?

By gradually taking all of these decisions, the non-Christian is nudged closer and closer to commitment until the time arrives when he is ready to take the step. We should not assume that he will do it as quickly as we imagine. Nor that we must be around when it happens. God can bring a lot of different resources into the situation to complete the work he has started; we should be content to be part of the process.

Jim Smith, a distinguished Anglican evangelist, once wrote:

> Few people, if any, are converted instantly. They have moved through a number of stages, over a number of years. If you lead them to Christ, you can rejoice, but almost certainly someone else has done the donkey work . . .
>
> Once I was always worried that no one would respond to my preaching. It made me feel a failure. Then I realized that perhaps many had responded—they had moved along the sequence—but no one on that particular occasion was ready to move into the Response sequence. (Jim Smith, *Operation Breakthrough*, CPAS.)

However, *somebody* has to be there when the non-Christian takes his final 'mini-decision' and moves into 'the Response sequence'; and sometimes God will want that someone to be you! So how do we recognise when the time has arrived? The notebook suggests five principles.

First, *no one can respond until he has understood what he is responding to*. Well, sometimes people come to Christ with only the least glimmer of understanding of what the Gospel involves, and are soundly converted; but generally it's wrong to try to lead anyone to Christ before you're absolutely convinced that he knows what you are asking him to do.

Second, *no one can respond until he has counted the cost*. Jesus often seems to have tried his level best to deter people from following him! You might want to read the group passages such as Luke 9:57–62 or 18:18–22, and ask: was Jesus being unkind? (No, he wasn't; it would have been *really* unkind of him to tie those people down to a decision for which they were not personally prepared.) If you rush somebody through the gates of the Kingdom before he has fully appreciated the implications for his life, you will produce a still-born five-minute-wonder, not a genuine new creation.

No one can respond unless he is given a chance. Often through embarrassment we share our message with friends on a theoretical, abstract level, but shy away from making it personal: 'Isn't this something *you* should make a decision about?' But sooner or later people have to be given an opportunity to respond. Otherwise they can carry on forever nervously postponing the moment! It means that we have to take our courage in both hands and ask them—which is nerve-wracking. But if we *don't*, we're waiting instead for *them* to take *their* courage in both hands and broach the subject with *us*! Now is that fair?

People respond to open-ended questions. If you ask 'Do you want to become a Christian? and he says 'No'—out of embarrassment, or any other reason—you have effectively closed the door and made it much more difficult for yourself to raise the subject again. If instead you ask, 'Have you reached the point yet in your understanding of Christianity when you're ready to commit yourself to following Jesus?' you hold the door open for the future—by implying that if he isn't there yet, he may be someday. It makes it natural for you to re-open the subject later if the answer is 'No'. And because it sounds a less threatening, less point-blank question, you won't get so many 'Noes' anyway; people won't back away through fear but will give you a thoughtful, frank answer.

People do not respond when pushed. If you sense reserve or hesitancy to answer, back off. Change the subject tactfully. (That in itself will take your witness to him one step further: you will communicate the message, 'I'm not a scalp-hunter. I respect your independence as a person.') If you have presented your message to the very best of your ability, and you are confident that he understands but is reluctant to respond, it does no harm to say, 'Well, the ball's in your court now. Contact me when you're ready to decide about these things.' If God is at work, you will be contacted!

When you sense that your friend needs more time to consider the implications of deciding for himself, you may find it useful to introduce him to an 'Agnostics Anonymous' or 'Just Looking' group in which he can learn more without any pressure or embarrassment (see *Back-up material* section). Jim Petersen's book contains an outline of how to conduct a personal Bible study with a non-Christian; that could be another alternative.

Sometimes non-Christians who have several Christian friends find it difficult to say openly, 'I have become a

Christian'—just in case it doesn't work out and they are left
feeling that they have disappointed and let down their
friends! I have sometimes suggested to such people that they
should begin quietly reading a Bible passage and spending
time in prayer each day, asking Jesus to become real to them,
committing themselves to do whatever their Bible passage
told them to do, obediently and without question. God
answers the prayers of those who are honestly looking for
him, and I have invariably found that within a month such
people are so confident of their new relationship with Jesus
that they don't mind telling anybody about it!

After discussing each of these principles, end with EXER-
CISE 3.

EXERCISES

EXERCISE 1: Divide the group into pairs. Ask one member of
each pair to pretend he is talking to another Christian, not a
member of the group, who has just asked the question, 'What
have you been doing on this course?' Let them talk for a
minute or two, then change it. Ask them to pretend that the
other person is not a Christian, but a non-Christian, who has
just asked the same question. Most group members will
admit afterwards that they found it much more difficult to
answer second time round! Why do we get so scared, and
sound so unnatural, when talking to unbelievers?

OR: Get 3 of the more experienced members of the group to
talk about occasions when they fluffed chances to talk about
Jesus (the more humorous the story, the better!) Ask the rest
of the group if they have had similar experiences. Ask why
we act this way.

OR: Ask the group to answer the following questions in
writing, very honestly:

If a casual acquaintance (not a close friend) remarked to
you, 'What did you do last night?', and you'd been to a
prayer meeting, would you:

(a) Say, 'I went to a prayer meeting.'
(b) Say, 'Uh . . nothing much . . .'
(c) Say, 'You wouldn't be interested. What did you do?'
How many close friends do you have to whom you have explained the Gospel?
How many close friends do you have to whom you have not explained the Gospel?
How long could someone know you without realising what a Christian is?

Then discuss the reasons for the fears which keep us from witnessing.

EXERCISE 2: In small groups, share the most persuasive lies the Devil tells you, and which of the six ideas you need to work on next week; and pray together for what each person has shared.

OR: Get individuals to write down for themselves:

MY MAJOR PROBLEM WITH BOLDNESS IS . . .
ACTION I NEED TO TAKE IS . . .
WITH GOD'S HELP, THIS WEEK I WILL . . .

OR: In small groups, discuss the most important personality gifts which God has given to each member, which can be of use in witnessing. (Examples: one very shy girl may nonetheless have a gift for listening to problems and sympathising with people in distress; a less sensitive boy may have enough confidence and natural nerve to open up conversations where others wouldn't dare; someone very intelligent may be able to handle reasoned arguments about the faith better than the others; and so on.) When people see themselves through the eyes of the others, they may begin to appreciate more readily what God has given them, and which sides of their personality they need to work at, to make themselves of maximum effectiveness in evangelism.

EXERCISE 3: Get group members to think back to the time

before they became Christians. If they had to identify the six most important mini-decisions they made before accepting Christ—what would they be? Compare results, and see if the exercise helps you to understand better the stages people commonly go through before clinching their decision. (Note: those who were born into Christian families, or became Christians at such a young age that they can hardly remember being unconverted, will find this exercise difficult! For them it might be more realistic to think about someone they know who has become a Christian within the last few years. What stages did that person appear to go through? Failing all else, you could have them read through a few 'testimony' stories in a Christian paperback or an evangelistic newspaper such as *Challenge* or *Emergency Post*, and identify the 'mini-decisions' which the subjects of the stories made as they came closer and closer to commitment.)

OR: There are many 'put-off' comments which non-Christians can make to discourage a Christian: 'Oh, I'm not really interested in religion', 'Well, it's fine if you want to believe in it, but I think you should live and let live', 'I think religion is a private personal matter and I don't discuss my views'. Get one half of the group to work out a selection of such comments, and then let the others try to talk to them about Jesus. See if the second group can work out effective ways of working round the 'put-offs' devised by the first. (Then, if time allows, switch roles between the two groups).

OR: Divide into smaller groups to try to work out an original *series of questions* which could be used (a) to begin a natural conversation about Jesus (b) to ask a friend gently whether he is yet read to accept Jesus as Lord. One example of (a), suggested by Leroy Eims, is:

'Are you interested in spiritual matters?'

'Have you ever considered becoming a real Christian?'

'If someone were to ask you what a real Christian is—what would you say?'

The answer to the first two questions can be 'Yes' *or* 'No'—it doesn't matter! The next question still follows quite logically! And the third question launches you very naturally into a discussion of the basic issues.

Share the results of different groups, and note down any good ideas.

VISUALS

The two diagrams in the student notebook.

BACK-UP MATERIAL AND FURTHER READING

Anything on the subject of *Christian courage*—such as biographies of timid people whom God used—could be a useful resource. Your local Christian bookshop will advise.

We have already mentioned the books by Leroy Eims and Jim Petersen which are mentioned in *Explanation of content*. Jim Smith's booklet *Breakthrough: A Theory of Teenage Evangelism* is published by Church Pastoral Aid Society. *Emergency Post* can be ordered from Paternoster Press, publishers of this book; as well as a source of interesting stories, you can use it as a resource for your members to hand on to non-Christian friends—to encourage them to begin getting involved in evangelism.

Joseph Aldrich's *Life-Style Evangelism* (Marshall), which we have referred to before, has a section (Chapter 11) containing some useful ideas on the subject of *beginning conversations* without manipulation, embarrassment or insensitivity. Aldrich suggests a very effective sequence of questions and statements which anyone can use.

Just Looking—a series of non-embarrassing group meetings for young people who are exploring Christianity but have not yet reached the point of commitment—is published by Bible Society. The author is John Allan.

HOMEWORK

Before next time, ask the group members to try to begin a conversation about the Gospel with someone they know.

They should pray first! In fact, they may want to choose one of the three people for whom they have been specifically praying. They should report back next time on what happens.

WORKSHOP 8

Making the Big Introduction

AIM OF SESSION

(1) To give group members confidence that they could introduce someone to Christ
(2) To teach them one method of doing so

OUTLINE OF SESSION

'Some lessons from Ananias' (BIBLE STUDY)
|
OPEN PRAYER
|
'One logical method' (down to 'Important Question No. 2')
|
EXERCISE 1
|
'One logical method' (the remaining part)
|
EXERCISE 2

EXTRA PREPARATION

Write out some slips of paper giving instructions for EXERCISE 2. For EXERCISE 1, you may wish to give two group members the script of a sketch to prepare (see page 86), and possibly run off several copies of the sketch, one for each group member. (Again, permission to photocopy this page is included in the purchase of the book).

EXPLANATION OF CONTENT

(1) *Some lessons from Ananias*

God can use any Christian to lead someone else to Christ. Ananias of Damascus was never very famous, but he is one of the most strategic people in the New Testament—without him, the Apostle Paul could not have become a Christian. Read the story in Acts 9:10–19, and have a group Bible study on it, using the following questions for discussion. (If you have a large group, you may wish to divide it into smaller groups for the discussion. That probably means allowing some of your more experienced members to lead the discussion groups, since you can't be everywhere at once; make sure they have a copy of the questions well beforehand.)

1. Ananias responded 'Here I am' when he hear God's voice (v. 10). How might a different Christian have reacted? How would *you* react in the same circumstances? What does it tell you about the kind of people God uses to bring others to faith?

2. Why would no one but Ananias do for this job (v. 11)? Does this suggest anything about the kind of jobs God might entrust to us?

3. Do you think Ananias felt confident in his ability to do the job (vv. 13–14)? What lessons can we learn from this?

4. How did the Lord deal with Ananias' fears (vv. 15–16)? How could he deal with ours in a similar way?

5. What do you think was the importance of the first two words Ananias said to Saul (v. 17)? What else could he have begun with?

6. Look at Acts 22:16. What *else* does it teach you about Ananias' methods which doesn't appear in ch. 9?

As a group, decide what important lessons you have learned from this passage. Then spend time together praying over them, asking God to build into the lives of each of you the qualities he found in Ananias.

(2) *One logical method*

Stress that there is no magic formula for bringing people to faith, but that what the notebook outlines is just one way of doing it . . .

How do you help someone meet Jesus? You could be helping someone well known to you, or a total stranger, at the end of an evangelistic meeting; either way, make sure first that the person concerned is at his ease (as Ananias did). If he is a stranger, find out his name if necessary; ask a couple of questions (e.g. about his job, family, home area) which show an interest in him, and also allow him to start the easy way—with questions he doesn't find it too difficult to respond to! Then ask IMPORTANT QUESTION NO. 1— never assume you know what he's there for: he may just be confused, or he may have a family problem which he vaguely feels God might help him with, or he might even be looking for the toilet and have wandered into the wrong room by mistake!

If on the other hand you are dealing with a friend of yours, who has just reached the point of admitting his need of Christ after many conversations with you, QUESTION NO. 1 will be unnecessary since you know exactly what the situation is already. But all the same, take care not to embarrass him! You could *panic* ('Oh, help, this is the big one, this is what I've been praying for, what do I do now?') or *become excited* and start turning cartwheels ('Yippee! yippee! he said it! he said it!') or cover your excitement by adopting a *falsely casual* tone. None of these reactions will put the other person at his ease! Be natural, straightforward and frank.

Having established that he wishes to become a Christian, check to make sure he knows the basic facts (GOD, SIN, JESUS, FAITH); explain each and ask a question which will show you whether or not he has understood, before moving on to the next. (For example, after talking about *sin* you could ask: 'So what do you think is God's opinion of us?') When

you are convinced he knows the facts, ask without embarrassment IMPORTANT QUESTION NO. 2. Remember,
nothing is as infectious as embarrassment; if you become
awkward and unnatural, he will be embarrassed too, and shy
away from making a decision. So ask him clearly and plainly:
'What are you going to do?' That's what Ananias did.

(Here do EXERCISE 1 then continue.)

There are 3 possible answers to the question.
NOTHING: if he decides not to proceed to commitment,
we don't have the right to nag him into doing so. All we can
do is remind him of the 3 things the Holy Spirit uses to
convince people of the truth of the Gospel (John 16:8)—sin,
the PAST problem of forgiveness, which will never be
achieved without Christ; righteousness, the PRESENT problem of inability to live right, which will never be possible
without Christ; and judgement, the FUTURE problem of
escaping God's wrath, which will never be possible without
Christ. But if we remind him of these things, and he still
elects to refuse, we must allow him to go. Jesus never clung
on to anyone. He respected individual freedom.
WAIT: if he decides to go away and think about it, again
that's his privilege. But ensure that he *does* think about it by
arranging to meet him for a further talk within 48 hours. You
could also leave him something to read to focus his thinking.
All this will just remind him that a decision needs to be made,
sooner or later.
ACCEPT CHRIST: if this is his decision, *make sure* he is
introduced to Christ. The exact means is not important—you
might pray for him, and get him to say 'Amen' at the end;
you might ask him to pray, phrase by phrase, following you;
in some circumstances he might wish to pray by himself—the
important thing is that this person and Jesus come face to
face, and a genuine commitment is made between them. The
prayer could take any form, but should stress what the new
Christian is doing—admitting sin, asking for forgiveness,
inviting Jesus Christ to take command.
If you feel unsure of your ability to pray out loud
spontaneously, you will find 'model' prayers in many
evangelistic leaflets and books. The easy thing to do is to turn

to one of those and read it out. But it has the drawback of seeming a bit artificial and impersonal. A good compromise is to make up your own ideal prayer (using those in the leaflets as a model if you wish!) and write it in your Bible. Then, when you need to use it with someone, you can simply find it and explain that this is such a special moment that you have written a prayer especially for this precise situation. In this way, your prayer can seem quite personal and original—as it should!—but you won't face the anxiety of having to think out what to say on the spur of the moment.

After the prayer, it's amazing how many people expect to feel something unusual happening inside them. So IMPORTANT QUESTION NO. 3 can be worth asking. Whether they answer *Yes* or *No*, it gives you a chance to explain that faith must not be built upon feelings, but upon the clear promises of God in the Bible. Give the new Christian a couple of verses to look at and remember. (Get your group members to suggest verses which might be useful here.) Feelings come and go; God's promises are timeless.

Finally, *make sure* (as Ananias did) that the new Christian will be helped to grow up afterwards. Ideally, you should be doing the job yourself; if this is impossible, ensure that he is introduced personally *and without delay* to someone who is willing to supervise his growth as a Christian, and befriend him. (Make sure someone—preferably you—contacts him within 24 hours to see how his first day as a new Christian has gone.) We'll look at what's involved in caring for a new Christian in our next workshop.

EXERCISES

EXERCISE 1: In pairs, explain the Gospel to one another point by point, asking a question after each point which allows you to see whether the other person has understood what you are saying.

OR: Practice the skill of listening to someone else. Divide into groups of five; one person asks the other four questions about a mythical person, Tony Williams, whom they are all supposed to know. He can ask any question he likes, of any member of the group; but all the answers they give (although they're making them up on the spot) must agree with one another. If any group member gives an answer which conflicts with something which has already been said, he drops out. The game continues till every one of the four has made a mistake, or the questioner runs out of questions; it supplies practice in listening closely to what other people are saying—something most of us do very rarely, but a vital skill in helping someone find Christ. What they say provides the verbal clues which help us work out how best to take them further. (With younger or less imaginative groups, have two questioners instead of one—or supply them with some specimen ideas for questions to ask.)

OR: Get two group members to act out the sketch shown below.

CHRISTIAN: Hello, hello, do sit down. So you want to be a Christian, do you? Good. Well, the first thing you need to know . . .

NON-CHRISTIAN: Well, actually, that wasn't what I . . .

CHRISTIAN: Oh, no! How silly. I forgot! Name, address, date of birth. Quickly now.

NON-CHRISTIAN: Hey—that's a bit personal, isn't it?

CHRISTIAN: Oh, all right, no offence meant. Let me tell you how to be a Christian, then.

NON-CHRISTIAN: But I don't really . . .

CHRISTIAN: Please don't interrupt! Now, where was I? Oh, yes. You were created by God. You believe in God, don't you?

NON-CHRISTIAN: Now that's something I've never really been sure about . . .

CHRISTIAN: . . . Yes, I'm sure you do really. Anyway. God created you and gave you freewill but you turned your back on him so Jesus came down to the cross to die and bring you new life. Hmmm. Yes, that's about it. That covers the basic facts. You understood that?

NON-CHRISTIAN: No, I . . .

CHRISTIAN: Good, good, I'm so glad. Well, now I have to ask you an embarrassing question. A dreadfully embarrassing question. You won't get embarrassed, will you? I hate this bit. Will you—what I mean is—umm—would you—that is—do you want to accept Christ now?

NON-CHRISTIAN: No, I've been trying to tell you. That's my coat you're sitting on, and I want to go home. Can I have it back now?

CHRISTIAN: Oh! Oh . . . of course . . . hey, wait a minute, Mr . . . What did you say your name was?

NON-CHRISTIAN (*on the way out*): You never asked.

Ask the rest of the group how many mistakes they noticed (I think there are eleven!). Discuss them together. If you think it will help the discussion, give them each a copy of the script to consult. (But don't issue these copies until they have seen the sketch acted out.)

EXERCISE 2: Pretend that you are all in the 'counselling room' at the end of an evangelistic event. Give half of the group members slips of paper containing details of the role you want them to play (e.g. 'You are 21, a student of electrical engineering, with a Christian mother, and you want to find Christ for yourself'; 'You are 16, still at school and you are really just looking for a friend whom you thought was in the counselling room, but you are too embarrassed to say so'; 'You are 18, working in a shop, and you want to find Christ but cannot express your wishes very clearly. You do not understand the Gospel at all'; etc.). These members will be counselled by the others on a one-to-one basis. Then give the 'counsellors' slips of paper, switch the roles, and do it the other way round.

OR: Select three people to form a panel to answer questions from the rest, beginning 'What would you do if he said . . .' When anyone gives an unsatisfactory answer (let the whole group vote on it), he leaves the panel and his place is taken by the person who asked that question.

OR: Get group members to write out the kind of prayer they might pray with someone who wanted to find Christ. They should then learn the main lines of it, or else write it in their Bible (as suggested above).

VISUALS

Make a large copy of the flow-chart in the student notebook (it appears under the heading 'One logical method'). Keep it covered up, and uncover each part as you are talking about it.

BACK-UP MATERIAL AND FURTHER READING

You might want to study the three chapters containing the story of Paul's conversion (Acts 9, 22 and 26). You may need to do some reading on *assurance*, and the place of feelings in the Christian life. Some possible titles would be Michael Green, *New Life New Lifestyle* (Hodder); John Allan, *Sure Thing* (Kingsway); John White, *The Fight* (IVP). A book which is written for non-Christians, but can give Christians a superb model of how to deal sensitively with those who are at the point of deciding, is David Day's *This Jesus* (IVP)—especially the closing chapters of it.

HOMEWORK

If group members have not already done so, get them to work out a prayer they could pray with someone accepting Christ, and either learn it by heart or write it in their Bibles. Also, ask them to think of three people who had an especially important impact upon their spiritual development as Christians; and to jot down some ideas about what it was that made such an impact.

WORKSHOP 9

Making a Disciple

AIM OF SESSION

(1) To show the need for after-care of new Christians
(2) To create an understanding of what is needed in after-care
(3) To teach the group the basic activities which lead to growth.

OUTLINE OF SESSION

Introduction
|
EXERCISE 1
|
'Being a parent involves . . .'
|
'Look what Jesus did for his disciples!'
|
'How a new Christian needs to grow'
|
EXERCISE 2
|
'The basics of growth'
|
EXERCISE 3

EXPLANATION OF CONTENT

(1) *Introduction*

A new Christian has been 'born again' (John 3:3) into a strange new world, and like any other baby he needs lots of help in growing up. Look at the references given in the student notebook, then go straight into EXERCISE 1.

(2) *Being a parent involves . . .*

Ask members to list on a piece of paper the major things their parents did for them to help them grow up. You should end up with a list including the four items mentioned in the student notebook. Discuss how a *spiritual* parent could do these things for his 'child'. Look at 1 Thess. 2:7, 1 Pet. 2:2, Acts 20:20, Phil. 3:17.

(3) *Look what Jesus did for his disciples!*

Examine the five things listed. Can the group think of examples of these things in the Gospels? (Just in case they can't, you'd better think out examples beforehand!) How will these things affect the way we bring up spiritual 'children'?

(4) *How a new Christian needs to grow*

The human personality has three parts—MIND, WILL and EMOTIONS—*each* of which must grow if the new Christian's life is to be well-balanced. (Too much concentration on MIND, and he'll have a strong grasp of doctrine, but a poor personal life. Too much stress on WILL, and he'll be a joyless disciplinarian. Too much stress on EMOTIONS, and he'll be a superficial convert with fluctuating enthusiasm.)

What needs to happen to each area of the new Christian's personality?

* With his MIND, he needs to *learn to learn*—to find out what the faith is all about, to wrestle with his understanding of the Christian message, to saturate his memory with God's Word.

* With his EMOTIONS, he needs to *learn to love*—to worship and appreciate the Lord Jesus, to relax in the security of belonging to God's family, to share love with others in the family.

* With his WILL, he needs to *learn to live*—to withstand temptation, to put Jesus first, to establish an unselfish, caring Christian lifestyle, to keep calm under pressures and problems.

EXERCISE 2 should follow at this point.

(5) *The basics of growth*

Four absolutely vital activities are the key to growing spiritually:

USING THE BIBLE—at first the Bible will probably seem a very daunting book (it's long, it's from a long time ago, and it's divided up in a confusing way). To many people, a Bible is something you're given at Confirmation, something you swear on in a court of law, something to be solemnly read out on official public occasions—not a book you can actually *read*. And so it will take time to help a new Christian understand the different things which can be done with the Bible: reading a passage every day; reading through a whole book at a time; studying a section in detail; memorizing important verses; hearing it discussed and preached about. Part of your job as a spiritual 'parent' is to introduce these activities to him gradually, remembering that if he's not used to much reading anyway he will be easily frightened of too many intellectual challenges.

PRAYER—a new Christian needs to be shown how to organise a prayer time on his own, how to join a prayer meeting with others, how to pray for specific needs he has, and how to begin praying regularly for the needs of others. This means you must spend a lot of time praying with him, showing him how to do it and encouraging him to grow in confidence.

WITNESS—new Christians are both the *best* and *worst* witnesses there are, says Jim Petersen (*Evangelism for our*

Generation, pp. 157–9; read the book to find out what he means!). The 'best' side of it is that they tend to have a social circle mostly consisting of unconverted people. After a few months, their pattern of relationships will have changed; they'll be spending more of their time in Christian activities, and some of those contacts may have gone forever. So encourage him as soon as possible to IDENTIFY HIMSELF by letting his friends know, very quietly, what has happened to him; then when his courage grows to INVITE his friends to places where they will meet Christians and perhaps hear the Christian message; then to begin to ANSWER THEIR QUESTIONS; then finally to TAKE THE INITIATIVE and start positively sharing his new-found faith.

FELLOWSHIP—He needs to develop different *levels* of fellowship. He needs a ONE TO ONE relationship with someone extremely supportive, whom he can trust (you); he needs to feel at home in a SMALL GROUP where he can ask questions, feel wanted, and share deeply with a few others; he needs to be identified with a CHURCH CONGREGATION where he can learn from good teaching and get involved in the church's work; and finally it's good to be part of a LARGE CELEBRATION occasionally, for encouragement and inspiration. If the group members think about how these different levels have contributed to their own Christian experience, they will begin to understand what you are talking about. Get them to work out how they could build these different levels of fellowship into a new disciple's life, in their own church and situation.

Stress finally that all of this is just introductory stuff—a way of starting the new disciple off in the right direction. There is much more to be learned about helping a new Christian to grow, stage by stage. And some of that will be the subject of the final workshop.

EXERCISES

EXERCISE 1: In groups of three, share with one another

details of the people who have had most impact on your spiritual development (see last time's *Homework*). Why was that? What does it tell you about making disciples?

OR: Discuss in small groups: 'The one thing I wish somebody had told me, when I first became a Christian, is . . .' What are the vital things new Christians must be told?

OR: Look at 1 Thessalonians 2 for ideas on what's involved in being a spiritual parent. How many ideas can you find?

EXERCISE 2: Get people to write down their own private answers to these questions:
  * Which is my weakest area spiritually—mind, will, emotions?
  * What can I do to strengthen that area?
  * What can I do about it *this week*?

Get them to share their answers with just one group member (but keeping private anything they don't want to reveal) and to pray with that other person for one another.

OR: In groups of three or four, draw up a list of activities which would contribute to a new Christian's growth in each area—learning to live, love, learn. Compare results.

OR: Decide how you could help each of these cases:

(a) a new Christian who loves sessions of praise and worship, but gets depressed easily, has little understanding of the Scriptures, and seems unable to keep a daily time of prayer and Bible study going consistently;

(b) a new Christian whose moral life is scrupulously pure but who keeps falling out with those whose political or religious views differ slightly from his own;

(c) a new Christian with a firm grasp of the Scriptures and a warm, loving personality, who is however sleeping with his girlfriend and seems unwilling to stop.

EXERCISE 3: Share in small groups how the four basic activities (Bible use, prayer, witness, fellowship) have helped *you* grow personally. What was the biggest discovery you ever made about each of these?

OR: In pairs, pretend that one partner is a new Christian. Then have a discussion about the value of one of the four basic activities. The 'new Christian' should ask, 'Why should I?' and try to come up with all the problems and difficulties a new Christian might raise. The other person should try to answer all the questions raised, giving illustrations from his own experience, and helpful verses from the Bible when appropriate. Then switch roles and discuss another of the four activities.

OR: Get each group member to answer the following questions on a piece of paper:

* Looking at my own performance with the four basic activities—how would I grade myself, from 0 to 5, in each area?

* Where do I need to improve?

* Do I need to ask anyone's advice or help?

* What should my first move be, *this week*?

Conclude the workshop with a time of open prayer in which people can ask God for help in the ways they have identified—and can pray for everybody else as well.

VISUALS

See diagram opposite.

BACK-UP MATERIAL
AND FURTHER READING

Passages which contain ideas about *making disciples* could be worth studying (e.,g. Acts 20, 1 Timothy 4, 2 Corinthians 6). And of course there are lots of books on the process of *growing as a Christian*: apart from those we have already mentioned (p. 88), there is a whole series of brief paperbacks published by Scripture Union, under the title 'Moving on', dealing with individual aspects of Christian growing up: prayer, the Bible, the church, temptation, guidance, and so on.

There are a few good *after-care courses* which can help Christians to meet regularly with new disciples, in order to

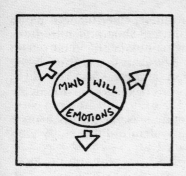

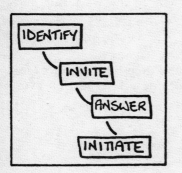

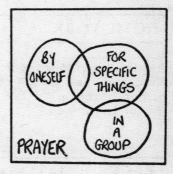

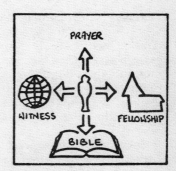

pray and study together and encourage growth. Get some samples from your local Christian bookshop and introduce them to the group. There is a growing number of resources to help people start *making sense of the Bible* for themselves: I like the *Bible User's Starter Kit* from Lion, and the *Know Your Bible* series of daily Bible study workbooks from IVP.

Good books on *how to look after a new Christian* aren't so easy to find, though there are lots of good ideas in David Watson's *Discipleship* (Hodder), including a system of Bible study you can use with a new Christian. Gary Kuhne's *The Dynamics of Personal Follow-Up* (Zondervan) has a wealth of practical insights, although his method is a little too schematic and organized to work with everybody.

HOMEWORK

Ask the group to revise everything they have learnt so far. Next time, the workshop will include a brief test on every part of the course.

WORKSHOP 10

Helping the Baby Grow

AIM OF SESSION

(1) To show members how they can develop the spiritual life of a new Christian.
(2) To give a clear understanding of what 'maturity' is—the goal of the discipling process.

OUTLINE OF SESSION

'Meeting him regularly'
|
EXERCISE 1
|
'Dangers to avoid'
|
EXERCISE 2
|
'What "maturity" means'
|
EXERCISE 3
|
FINAL TEST

EXTRA PREPARATION

You may have decided which materials you want your members to use in conducting simple Bible studies with new Christians; if so, have some copies available to pass on to them. You may wish to write your own, if you can't find anything suitable.

You should prepare several copies of the maturity/immaturity scales (see below under EXERCISE 3)—at least one for each group member.

EXPLANATION OF CONTENT

(1) *Meeting him regularly*

The most important part of one-to-one discipling is the regular (preferably weekly) meeting between the new Christian and the person who is him. It shouldn't go on for too long—an hour or just over is fine—and you should not give in to temptation to go on talking on all night. If you end it while he's still interested, he'll come back eagerly for more; but after one or two marathon sessions he will easily lose interest. Fix a time and stick to it—if you keep changing details of time and venue, one of you is sure to forget a meeting sooner or later.

Have the first meeting within two days of his acceptance of Christ. It's vital to stay close to him right at the start; the first few days of Christian living are often the toughest!

Within the meeting, include these elements:

* Simple *Bible study* of some truth he needs to learn, followed by a time of prayer together about any lessons you have learned from it.

* A *chat about the previous week*, since you last met—how is he getting on spiritually? Have there been problems, difficulties, discoveries, answered prayers? Talk about his progress, and pray about it all.

* Also, an *honest sharing* of *your* week—on anything God

has taught you, any mistakes you have made which he can learn from, and so on. Remember 1 Thess. 2:8.

* At the end, a *project* which you want him to complete over the next week which will allow him to try out some of the principles he has been learning in his own life. (For example, if your Bible study has been about love, you could ask him to go out and find a Christian he really finds it difficult to be friends with, and do something loving for that person—then report to you on the result. Or if you were studying answers to prayer, you could ask him to interview three older Christians about ways in which God has answered prayer in their lives, then to report the results to you. Anything which makes the Bible teaching more practical and real to him—and also anything which brings him into contact with more and more members of the church—is good.)

Now do EXERCISE 1.

(2) *Dangers to avoid*

(a) DON'T RUSH THINGS. Start slowly and carefully. Don't feel you *must* cover the whole of a topic in one session . . . take it at his speed. On the first occasion, you may do no more than explain exactly what is going to happen in future weeks, and have a simple prayer time with him. Speed can lead to misunderstanding—so keep it at a gentle pace!

(b) DON'T RELY SOLELY ON WEEKLY MEETINGS. Get to know him, his family, his interests, without being pushy or prying. Share activities with him, do things together.

(c) DON'T PRETEND TO BE MORE SPIRITUAL THAN YOU ARE. You can't take him any closer to the Lord than you have already come. If you pretend to be more of a Christian hero than you are, you're heading for embarrassment. He'll find out the truth about you before long!

(d) DON'T PRETEND INFINITE WISDOM. Where there are questions you can't answer:

—if you can find the answer for him, *admit you don't know*, then say, 'But I'll find out for next week.'

—if you can find out the answer while he's there (e.g. by looking up a reference book), show him how to do it. If he's perfectly able to find out the answer for himself, with a little bit of hard work, send him off to do it!

—if there are areas you can't handle—e.g. deep sexual, psychological or occult problems—know which older Christians you can turn to who will give expert help in such areas. (Why not get the group to try to construct a list of such people before you go any further?)

(3) *What 'maturity' means*

The Greek word *teleios* appears quite often in the New Testament. It is the word which means 'mature', although often in older translations it's rendered as 'perfect'. That's confusing, because no Christian will ever attain perfection in this life—point out to the group that Philippians 1:6 tells us that the good work which God has begun in us will not be complete till the day of Christ's return. However, we can all reach *maturity*, and in Col. 1:28 Paul says that the aim of his work with new Christians is 'to present every man *teleios* in Christ'.

Look with the group at the verses listed, and the traits of maturity which they tell us about. Then do EXERCISE 3 before concluding the course with the test.

A FINAL WORD   Remember to thank everyone for the hard work they have put in, and stress that this is not the end, but the beginning. Now comes the time to apply these principles in real life. You may have some specific project which will involve them in sharing their faith—e.g. a coming mission or series of meetings—and if so you should give details now, and tell them what you will be expecting them to do. Or you may just be expecting them to apply the contents of the course in their normal everyday lives; if so, it could be good to suggest that (a) the pairs who have been praying for specific people continue to do so regularly, and (b) you all get together again in four or five weeks' time to review progress in applying the principles, and pray together about all that has happened.

Remind them that in our century the church is growing as never before in history. It's happening because ordinary Christians are sharing their faith with acquaintances; not because of a few great evangelists or up-to-date communications gimmicks. The members of your group are now better equipped than ever before to be part of the greatest rescue mission on earth. Assure them that you will continue to pray for them individually, ask them to pray for one another, and remind them that they can come to you at any time they need help or advice in their job of making Jesus' message known.

EXERCISES

EXERCISE 1: Divide into pairs, and get them to plan out how they would spend an hour with a new Christian. 'The subject for Bible study is *the importance of the Bible*; this is your fourth meeting together. What passages would be most important to read together? What project could you set? How would you allocate the time?' Make sure that time is left for all the necessary activities—*including* some time for friendly chat at the start (after all, you can't just jump straight into Bible study!) and time to report back on last week's project.

OR: Get them to think through this last week. What have they learnt from God in the past seven days which it could be useful to share with a non-Christian? Let them discuss it in groups of two.

OR: Divide into small groups, and ask each group to draw up a list of the 12 subjects they would consider it most important to cover in Bible study with a new Christian. Compare results, and work out a 'master list' using the best suggestions from each group.

EXERCISE 2: Ask them to divide into smaller groups, and devise possible projects which they could set a new Christian to do on the following subjects:

Prayer for others   Temptation and victory
The church   Patience

EXERCISE 3: Give them a copy of the maturity/immaturity scales, the diagram on page 102 which charts a Christian's progress from new birth towards maturity in six areas:

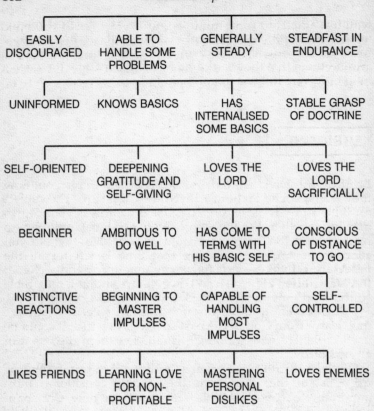

EASILY DISCOURAGED	ABLE TO HANDLE SOME PROBLEMS	GENERALLY STEADY	STEADFAST IN ENDURANCE
UNINFORMED	KNOWS BASICS	HAS INTERNALISED SOME BASICS	STABLE GRASP OF DOCTRINE
SELF-ORIENTED	DEEPENING GRATITUDE AND SELF-GIVING	LOVES THE LORD	LOVES THE LORD SACRIFICIALLY
BEGINNER	AMBITIOUS TO DO WELL	HAS COME TO TERMS WITH HIS BASIC SELF	CONSCIOUS OF DISTANCE TO GO
INSTINCTIVE REACTIONS	BEGINNING TO MASTER IMPULSES	CAPABLE OF HANDLING MOST IMPULSES	SELF-CONTROLLED
LIKES FRIENDS	LEARNING LOVE FOR NON-PROFITABLE	MASTERING PERSONAL DISLIKES	LOVES ENEMIES

Ask them to circle the points on the scale which they feel they have reached themselves. What can they do to improve their progress in the worst areas? Is there a project they could set themselves this week? Perhaps they could share their conclusions with one other group member, and then the two could pray for one another.

OR: Put a large copy of the maturity/immaturity scales on the overhead projector, and then put on top of it an overlay transparency which marks out circles round some of the points on the scale. Explain that this is a (fictional) picture of a new Christian's growth condition. Where is he doing best, and where worst? If you were looking after him, what would

you feel a need to concentrate on next? How could you build
in activities and challenges that might improve his performance in some of his weak areas? (If you prepare several
overlays—each giving a different picture—you could discuss
several fictional 'cases', one after another.)

VISUALS

A large copy of the maturity/immaturity scales could be
useful. And other main points could simply be written out on
overhead transparencies. But most of this session is practical
and participatory, so not much visual work is required.

BACK-UP MATERIALS AND FURTHER READING

Gary Kuhne's *The Dynamics of Discipleship Training* (Zondervan) contains some good material although it outlines a style
of training which will work better with some kinds of people
(the more intelligent, disciplined and idealistic) than with
others.

There are good books on *building relationships with others*:
Selwyn Hughes' *A Friend in Need* (Kingsway) is really about
helping people with their problems, but contains a lot of
useful advice for interpersonal friendships. Gene Getz,
Building up One Another (Victor) and Bruce Milne, *We Belong
Together* (IVP) discuss what Christians can do for one another,
while *Building with Bananas* by Derek and Nancy Copley
(Paternoster) is a very useful book about people problems in
the church.

On the subject of *growing towards maturity*, try John White,
The Race (IVP) and Charles Swindoll, *Strengthening your Grip*
(Hodder). A nineteenth-century classic on how Jesus trained
his disciples is *The Training of the Twelve* by Alexander B.
Bruce; if your church library doesn't have the original 1871
edition gathering dust somewhere, there are one or two

modern reprints of the work occasionally available through Christian bookshops (e.g. an American one from Keats Publishing, Inc., New Canaan, Connecticut).

And now, the test

Explain to the group that (a) the questions on pages N24f. are NOT a test that they can 'pass' or 'fail'. This is simply a method of reminding them, at the end of the course, of some of the subjects that have been covered; and of enabling them to assess how much of it all has stuck! And (b) this is NOT a test of how good or bad they will be in a real witnessing situation! It tests only one thing—their powers of mental recall—and there's much more to witnessing than that: the ability to relate to people, the ability to discern how much to say and when to say it . . . But it does no harm to end with a test like this, if only to let them see that they really have learned more than they imagine!

A final note

If your members have worked their way solidly through all ten workshops, it should not be long before the Lord entrusts them with the care of brand-new baby Christians to look after. Indeed, you may well have found some arriving already, while the course went through. When your members become involved in helping a new Christian, supervise them closely. Meet with them regularly to discuss progress; give them materials they can use in Bible study with the new Christian; always be available to cope with problems they may encounter. And before long, you may find yourself having to run this course of workshops again. For the next generation of brand-new Christians!

Course Notebook

WORKSHOP 1

EVANGELISM—DOING WHAT COMES NATURALLY

This workshop should help you understand what the Bible says about our role in recovering people for Jesus. And what we need if we're going to do the job properly.

EVANGELISM IS NATURAL

Is there a way in which we can share our faith completely NATURALLY, WITHOUT EMBARRASSMENT, without feeling we are imposing upon people, or making *them* feel they are being subjected to some artificial technique?

* Why *does the New Testament contain so few verses urging us to go out and evangelize?*

* Why *aren't there many accounts of how the early Christians went about the job of evangelism?*

* Why *does the Bible talk about two kinds of people—EVANGELISTS and WITNESSES?*

WHAT A 'WITNESS' IS

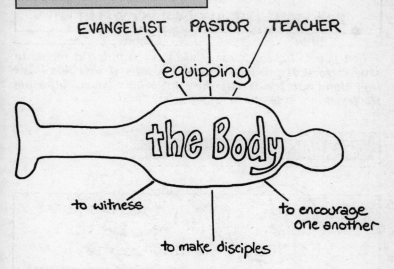

EVANGELIST   PASTOR   TEACHER

equipping

the Body

to witness

to make disciples

to encourage one another

WHAT A 'WITNESS' NEEDS

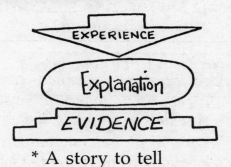

EXPERIENCE

Explanation

EVIDENCE

* A story to tell

* A jury to listen

* A reputation for honesty

WORKSHOP 2
PRAYER—THE SECRET INGREDIENT

When you're baking a cake, the most wonderful recipe in the world will produce dreadful results if you leave one ingredient out! It's exactly the same with recovering people for Jesus . . .

WHY DON'T WE PRAY MORE?

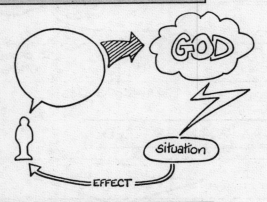

GET THE RIGHT PERSPECTIVE ABOUT PRAYER

- ☐ It's not just a *shopping list*

- ☐ It's not a way of *twisting God's arm*

- ☐ It's not a *super-holy feeling*

- ☐ It's not a way of *earning rewards*

FOCUS YOUR PRAYERS WITH INFORMATION

AGE	
OCCUPATION	
FAMILY	
INTERESTS	
RELATIONSHIP WITH YOU	
OPINION OF CHRISTIANITY	
MOST OBVIOUS NEEDS	
QUALITIES AND FAILINGS	
FEARS AND PRESSURES	

DO'S AND DONT'S

Don't:

dictate how God must
  answer
pray just 'when you feel
  like it'
let your faith go stale
keep your prayers safe
  and small

Do:

include praise and
  worship
pray 'faith-sized' prayers
pray that God will change
  your heart
pray continually
be ready to be changed

WORKSHOP 3
SHARING THE GOOD NEWS

This workshop should help you improve your skills in EXPLAINING CLEARLY what it is you believe . . .

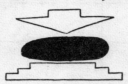

Without a good *explanation* of what you believe, your *experience* will seem subjective and your *evidence* will lead nowhere . . .

THE KEY POINTS OF THE GOSPEL

	VERSE	OBJECTION	ILLUSTRATION
1			
2			
3			
4			

USEFUL WAYS OF PRESENTING THE EXPLANATION

The bridge

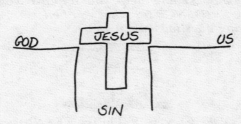

The 'Roman road'

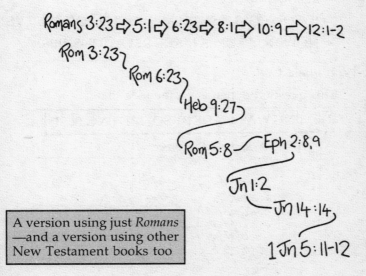

A version using just *Romans*
—and a version using other
New Testament books too

WORKSHOP 4
PRODUCING EVIDENCE FOR WHAT YOU SAY

This workshop should help you improve your skills in presenting EVIDENCE for what you believe . . . especially in answering questions about GOD.

Without EVIDENCE your EXPERIENCE will seem irrational — and your EXPLANATION will seem unrealistic

FOUR QUESTIONS ABOUT GOD

* *How can you believe in someone you can't see?*

    — SOMETIMES YOU HAVE TO

    — IF YOU *COULD* SEE HIM, WOULD YOU BELIEVE?

    — HOW DO PEOPLE MAKE RELATIONSHIPS?

* *Who made God?*

    This question depends on the idea that

EVERYTHING WAS MADE BY SOMETHING ELSE

When did this process begin?

NEVER? To say this is an act of faith not backed up by the facts

SOMETIME? ...so, you need an ultimate force to start it all off... God?

* *Would a God of love allow suffering?*

    — GOD DOESN'T LIKE IT EITHER

    — FREE WILL CAN BE MISUSED

    — RULES MUST BE KEPT

    — CREATION HAS BEEN SHATTERED

* *Why the Christian God?*

A MISLEADING PICTURE!

IF ALL ROADS LEAD TO GOD . . .

    none of them tell us much about him

    God can't care very much for us

    Christianity can't possibly be true

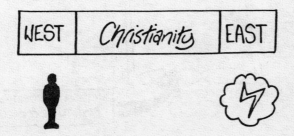

WORKSHOP 5
ARGUMENTS AND EVIDENCE

This workshop will help you improve your skills in answering eight questions non-Christians ask.

FOUR QUESTIONS ABOUT JESUS

* *Was he what the Bible claims?*

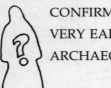

CONFIRMATION BY OTHER WRITERS

VERY EARLY MANUSCRIPTS

ARCHAEOLOGICAL EVIDENCE

* *Is the data trustworthy?*

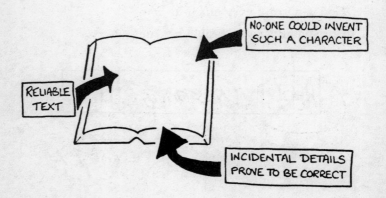

* Did he rise from the grave?

| MAYBE | *Someone stole the body—disciples, robbers, authorities?* |

| MAYBE | *he never died?* |

| MAYBE | *the whole thing was a legend?* |

* Was he just a good man?

1 He was undeniably a good man
2 But he claimed to be God!

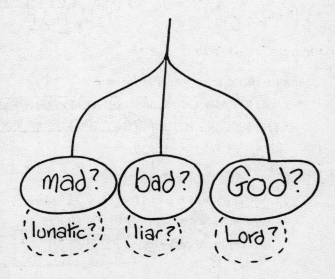

FOUR QUESTIONS ABOUT CHRISTIAN EXPERIENCE

* *Won't a good life do?*
  - ☐ WHAT IS 'GOOD'?
  - ☐ SO MUCH DEPENDS ON YOUR UPBRINGING
  - ☐ GOD ISN'T LOOKING FOR GOODNESS

* *Isn't it all imagination?*

You know it's
true by what
starts to happen . . .

* *What about those who haven't heard?*
  - — GOD IS <u>FAIR</u> AND UNWILLING TO CONDEMN
  - — GOD KNOWS HOW PEOPLE WILL RESPOND
  - — ROMANS 2

* *Hasn't science disproved it all?*
  - — READ THE BIBLE ON ITS OWN TERMS
  - — MANY SCIENTISTS BELIEVE IN GOD
  - — SCIENCE IS ANSWERING DIFFERENT QUESTIONS

FINALLY, REMEMBER . . .

* You can win an argument but lose your friendship with someone at the same time! Be tactful and gentle.
* Other people ask questions which aren't really important to them—just to cover up for the fact that they're getting very interested in your message, but don't want you to know!
* It is vital to learn how to switch from *defence* to *attack* in answering questions!

WORKSHOP 6
SHARING YOUR EXPERIENCE

We all need to learn how to talk about what has happened to us, in a way people can understand. This workshop should help you improve your skills in that area.

Without your EXPERIENCE your EXPLANATION will seem lifeless and your EVIDENCE will just be unreal theories.

WHAT CAN PREVENT YOUR STORY FROM BEING UNDERSTOOD?

* JARGON—using unintelligible words and phrases

* OVER MODESTY—feeling that you don't have much to tell

* EXAGGERATION—'improving' the facts of your story

* TOO MUCH CONTENT—trying to say too much and put too many theological points into it

* REPETITION—going round in circles because your story has no structure or plan

* IRRELEVANCE—concentrating on the unimportant bits

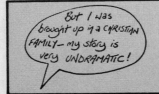

But I was brought up in a CHRISTIAN FAMILY—my story is very UNDRAMATIC!

SO WHAT?

. . . you can use it to make the point that all the religious upbringing in the world isn't enough to make you a Christian—a personal decision is still vital!

THE STRUCTURE OF YOUR STORY

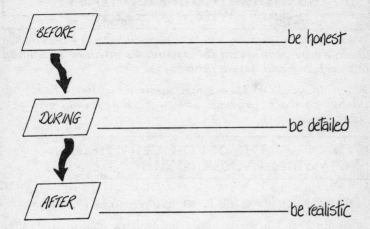

BEFORE _____ be honest

DURING _____ be detailed

AFTER _____ be realistic

HOW TO LEARN IT

1. Note down the <u>main points.</u>

2. Write out <u>one</u> of the parts of it <u>in full.</u>

3. Try it out on a Christian friend.

4. Try it out on a non-Christian friend.

5. Repeat the process.

WORKSHOP 7

KNOWING HOW MUCH TO SAY, AND WHEN TO SAY IT

Once we have mastered the basic skills involved in sharing our faith, we still have a problem.

When do we do it? How do we know when we're being too pushy—or too frightened? This workshop should give you some ideas.

DON'T LET THE DEVIL OVERWHELM YOU WITH FALSE GUILT

Here are some of the lies he sometimes tells Christians . . .

—'Every <u>real</u> Christian has a natural inclination to talk to everyone about it'

—'If you get it wrong, your friend could go to Hell!'

—'You'll make a mess of it. Then everyone will laugh at you.'

—'If you don't constantly talk to people about Jesus, you are a failure.'

—'You need to be clever, witty, theologically trained, full of resourcefulness and also very pushy.'

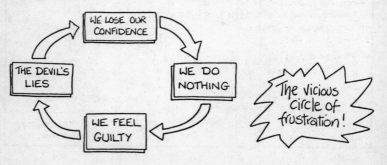

HOW TO DEVELOP YOUR BOLDNESS

Confess all that is wrong in your life

Take time to be with Jesus

Pray for boldness

Find a good example from whom you can learn, and who can inspire you

Fill your mind with God's Word

Don't wait for the perfect opportunity

HOW TO BEGIN A CONVERSATION —RECOGNIZING GOD'S TIME

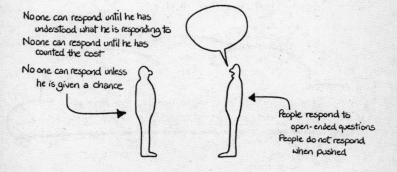

No one can respond until he has understood what he is responding to

No one can respond until he has counted the cost

No one can respond unless he is given a chance

People respond to open-ended questions

People do not respond when pushed

WORKSHOP 8
MAKING THE BIG INTRODUCTION

This workshop should help you learn the skill of introducing people to the Lord Jesus.

SOME LESSONS FROM ANANIAS

Here are some ideas you might pick up from this story . . .

* Be available to God for any task he chooses
* Remember that you are in a unique position with some people
* Fear can take away our usefulness for God
* Gain a clear picture of what God could do with this person's life
* Be open and welcoming
* Be confident
* Don't be afraid to challenge to decision
* Be available to help afterwards

ONE LOGICAL METHOD

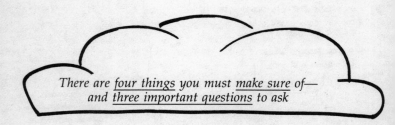

There are <u>four things</u> you must <u>make sure of</u>—
and <u>three important questions</u> to ask

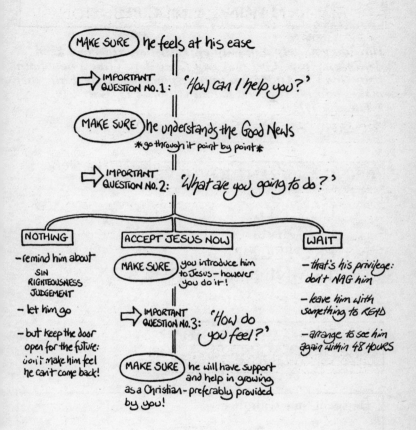

(MAKE SURE) he feels at his ease

▷ IMPORTANT QUESTION NO.1 : "How can I help you?"

(MAKE SURE) he understands the Good News
go through it point by point

▷ IMPORTANT QUESTION NO.2 : "What are you going to do?"

NOTHING

- remind him about
  SIN
  RIGHTEOUSNESS
  JUDGEMENT
- let him go
- but keep the door open for the future: don't make him feel he can't come back!

ACCEPT JESUS NOW

(MAKE SURE) you introduce him to Jesus – however you do it!

▷ IMPORTANT QUESTION NO.3 : "How do you feel?"

(MAKE SURE) he will have support and help in growing as a Christian – preferably provided by you!

WAIT

- that's his privilege: don't NAG him
- leave him with something to READ
- arrange to see him again within 48 HOURS

WORKSHOP 9
MAKING A DISCIPLE

How do you help a brand-new Christian become a keen disciple of Jesus Christ? A new Christian is like a new-born baby (John 3). And if you were responsible for the birth, that makes you his spiritual parent (1 Cor. 4:15, Gal. 4:19, 1 Thess. 2:11) . . .

BEING A PARENT INVOLVES . . .

LOVING
FEEDING
PROTECTING
TRAINING and EDUCATING

LOOK WHAT JESUS DID FOR HIS DISCIPLES!

He spent time with them

He made plans for them

He prayed for them

He gave them constant new challenges and tasks

He took them with him

HOW A NEW CHRISTIAN NEEDS TO GROW

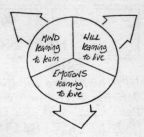

THE BASICS OF GROWTH

 USING THE BIBLE

Remember:

> * there are lots of different ways of using the Bible
>
> * introduce new Christians <u>gently</u> and <u>gradually</u>
>   —don't ask too much too soon

2 PRAYER

— on one's own
— in a small prayer group
— with the whole church

3 WITNESS—new Christians can sometimes be the most effective witnesses!

| IDENTIFYING ONESELF | INVITING TO EVENTS | ANSWERING QUESTIONS | TAKING THE INITIATIVE |

 FELLOWSHIP

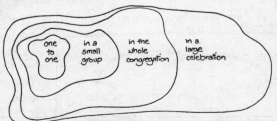

one to one • in a small group • in the whole congregation • in a large celebration

WORKSHOP 10
HELPING THE BABY GROW

This workshop should help you improve your skills in looking after a new Christian.

MEETING HIM REGULARLY

* Fix on a time and stick to it

* Study the Bible together

* Share your experiences with him

* Analyse his progress

* Set him projects to complete

Don't let your meetings go on beyond the agreed time!

DANGERS TO AVOID

Don't be in a rush—proceed at a speed he's comfortable with

Don't rely on weekly meetings alone

Don't pretend to be more spiritual than you are

* **PRAY** *about him*

* **RING HIM UP** *for a chat at times*

* **SPEND TIME** *with him in social, non-religious activities*

* **TAKE HIM WITH YOU** *to Christian events he will learn from*

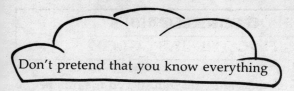

Don't pretend that you know everything

WHAT 'MATURITY' MEANS

The New Testament often uses the Greek word *teleios* to describe what it means to be 'mature' as a Christian. Here are a few examples:

MATTHEW 5:43:48 Someone who is able to love his enemies as well as his friends

JAMES 3:2 Someone who is able to control his impulses

PHILIPPIANS 3:15 Someone who is aware that he hasn't 'arrived' spiritually

MATTHEW 19:21 Someone who loves the Lord more than he loves himself

EPHESIANS 4:13–16 Someone who has a firm grasp of the basic doctrines of the faith

JAMES 1:2–4 Someone who can face trials and difficulties with steadfastness

HOW MUCH DO YOU REMEMBER?

(The number in brackets after each question is the number of the page in *Rescue Shop* where the answer appears.)

1. What is the New Testament word for someone who is not an evangelist? (12)

2. A witness has to have a STORY TO TELL, which involves knowing about three vital things. What are they? (13)

3. Give any one reason why Christians often don't pray as much as they should. (20)

4. How can you increase your ability to pray for others? (21)

5. What four facts form a good basis for an *explanation* of the Christian message? (31)

6. Draw the 'Bridge' diagram. (33)

7. What would the first verse be in your 'Roman Road' system? (32)

8. Name two of the key questions people ask about GOD. (42–4)

9. If all religions lead to God . . . what conclusions follow? Name any two of them. (44)

10. Give *one* answer to: 'Can you believe in someone you can't see?' (42)

11. Name *one* non-Christian writer who mentioned Jesus as a historical character. (50–1)

12. How many manuscripts of the New Testament do we have? (52)

13. Why is it impossible that grave robbers stole Jesus' body? Any one reason will do. (53)

14. Jesus was a good man, but claimed to be God. What three choices does that leave us, when we try to work out who he was? (54)

15. You know your faith isn't just wishful thinking because of what happens in three different areas of your life. Which? (55)

16. Which New Testament chapter says something about those who haven't heard the message? (56)

17. What three things should you do when you can't answer a question? (57)

18. What vital skill do we need to learn when answering questions? (57)

19. Name any three mistakes Christians make in telling their personal story. (64)

20. Name two lies the Devil tells us—and two ways of increasing our boldness. (73)

21. How do we recognise when someone has reached the point at which we can challenge him to accept Christ? We listed five principles. Can you name two? (74–5)

22. When leading someone to Christ, what do you do if he wants to go away and think it over? (84)

23. What are the three 'Important Questions' in helping someone meet Jesus? (83–5)

24. Which four basic activities lead to growth in a new Christian? (91–2)

25. Name *one* tell-tale sign of maturity. (100)